To whoever r
you be bless.
measure,

Ephesians 3:20

100
GOLD NUGGETS
OF WISDOM
FOR CHRISTIANS
TO RISE UP

DANIEL FLAGG

Acknowledgments

First I want to thank the Father, Son, and Holy Spirit for bringing this book forth so that others may rise up and experience the richer, fuller life God intends for all believers. I am grateful for the conviction placed on me to begin writing, the persevering spirit to continue in His timing, and the joy in my spirit present now as the writing has concluded.

I want to express my gratitude to my wife Lisa who saw my passion for this project and supported me through the years it took to bring it to print. Thank you Lisa for allowing me to devote hours on the manuscript that were above and beyond my regular work hours. Thank you for your support of the monetary outlays required for the project, especially after it was evident self-publishing would be necessary to bring it to fruition.

Finally greater glory was brought out of this manuscript by the group of editors who refined my thoughts to produce a more finished product. I thank God for bringing such talented editors to my assistance in just the right timing. Thank you Randy Peyser for helping me from the initial preparation of the manuscript and proposal and for guiding me through the entire process. Ms. Peyser introduced me to Cindy Chatham, who began the editing process when only a portion of the 100 nuggets had been written. I am grateful for Ms. Chatham's for putting the early nuggets on solid footing.

For the final editing I am grateful to a group of four editors who further refined and guided my work to the finished product. Thank you Angie Ramage, who gently refined my work and provided additional insight for this project via several phone conversations. Also to Anne Alexander who was a skilled editor and provided editing at a critical point during my writing. I am also grateful to have had a fellow church member and former high school classmate assist me in the editing process. This servant of God, Carol McLeod Jones, could only allocate a small portion of time due to her full time ministry work. I truly appreciate her friendship and the time she allocated to assist me in this process. The final editor I need to thank for all her work, guidance, compliments and insight is my own daughter, Megan. Megan you helped put all this together and I will forever be indebted to you for all your efforts. I love you so much and am grateful to have had you work alongside me (figuratively) in our home putting the finishing touches on this manuscript.

Introduction

Have you experienced those circumstances when God places something so heavily upon your heart that it moves you to action. We know God desires fellowship with us in spirit and truth and yet as we go about our life it sometimes takes a profound interruption for us to hear Him. This can occur such that we know without a doubt that the hand of God has reached out to touch us. There have been several times in my life where God convicted me so deeply that I was moved to respond and do something. One of those times was during devotion when I was praising God for the blessings in my life. In return I felt the press of God to respond by writing this book, to share some of the things with others that I was thanking God for at the time.

I thank God for His press, that He would communicate to me what He would desire of me, and it would be so compelling that it would move me into action. I grew up in a Christian home and have always been active in church but it wasn't until being born again in 2003 that I began to see significant changes occur in my life. He gave me an unquenchable desire for the Word and as I dug into the Word the result was positive changes in my life.

I was grateful to be part of a growing church where there were great biblical teachings and my family enjoyed worshipping. But my worship really went deeper when I started serving in this church. Our church opened a new campus in a nearby school where we would roll our equipment in and out each Sunday. This required arriving at 6 AM to set up and staying until 2 PM to tear down and remove the equipment. After arriving and beginning to serve at 6 AM I found myself in a great spiritual place when my family arrived at 9 AM for worship.

I believe God grows us in steps, and for me my spirituality went to the next level when I was asked to join the church prayer team. The prayer team would meet and pray for an hour or so before the 9 AM service. The prayer team leader was a great mentor and my prayer took on added dimensions as I listened, learned, and prayed. Just like practicing any sport, there is no substitute for putting yourself out there and praying, whether you feel the Holy Spirit with you or not, just keep praying.

The presence of the Holy Spirit is a powerful force and I experienced this powerful force on the day I began writing this book. It was February 28, 2014 when in my devotion time I felt the press of the Holy Spirit to write this book. I had my journal out and immediately started writing gold nuggets of wisdom that the Lord put swirling around in my head. I also wrote in my journal that "I will dedicate time to do this 6 days a week as of this date." I spoke to my wife that day about writing the book and she agreed that this was of God and that I should pursue it.

As I began writing I found myself studying the bible for more information. Also the Lord's confirmation and guidance was clearly evident which continued to fan the flames that the Holy Spirit ignited on February 28, 2014. But writing about 100 different spiritual topics while also working full time and attending to family issues was definitely challenging. As my home inspector workload increased during the summer and fall of 2014, I let a lapse develop in my writing of nuggets.

God is gracious and wants to bring to fruition what he begins in us and so by His grace on January 23, 2015 our senior pastor taught on "re-enlisting." During the sermon I was convicted that I had "dropped the ball" and that the timing of the teaching was an opportunity for me to begin again what the Holy Spirit had first laid on my heart.

I saw the work of God at hand as I continued to work on the writing. When the writing was far enough along to require an editor God put me in touch with an editor. When it was time for a cover design to be made, although I knew no graphic artist, the editor I was working with knew of a graphic artist who included in his work design of book covers. I could see God's hand at work at all stages of working on this project.

At different stages of writing this book I would let a few friends read a few of the nuggets. Their responses encouraged me and kept me on task. They were very complimentary and I understood that the words that I was writing were God filled words that He wanted others to experience. As I was writing God increased the creativity which He as our Creator bestows upon each of us and I would think of new and creative ways to reach readers through the gold nuggets.

Because the inspiration for this book came from the Holy Spirit, it goes without saying that the enemy does not want you to read this book. But if you are reading this you either have a copy of the book in front of you or are reading an electronic version. I encourage you to use this book to obtain the maximum benefit from it. If you are a structured reader you may do best reading the book beginning with Gold Nugget #1 and continuing sequentially through Gold Nugget #100. However one benefit of this book is that you can jump around from nugget to nugget starting with one in the middle of the book if you so desire, and then move to any other nugget.

The process of writing this book and having it printed has spanned a duration of almost five years. It has brought me great joy during this time to have studied the Word and to obtain a greater appreciation for our Lord and Savior, Jesus Christ. My walk with the Lord has grown immeasurably. I pray that you will be drawn closer to our Lord as you read through these "100 Gold Nuggets." Therefore I conclude with a prayer for you that the Lord would bless you as you spend time with "100 Gold Nuggets." And so Father, in the name of Jesus Christ I ask you to bless the reader of this book. I pray that these nuggets which you brought to my attention will serve a greater glory than mine alone. I pray Father that You will bring glory to each reader as they read these nuggets that they might be transformed by the nuggets and be drawn closer to You. I pray that the insight You have revealed to me will likewise be revealed at the appropriate time to each reader to further your Kingdom. In the name of Jesus I pray and believe. Amen

Contents

GOLD NUGGETS FOR SELF-IMPROVEMENT

GOLD NUGGETS CONCERNING GOD'S PROMISES

GOLD NUGGETS FOR FINANCIAL FREEDOM

Gold Nuggets to Increase Family Unity

1. Fight For Your Family

"Therefore I stationed some of the people behind the lowest points of the wall at the exposed places, posting them by families, with their swords, spears and bows. After I looked things over, I stood up and said to the nobles, the officials and the rest of the people, 'Don't be afraid of them. Remember the Lord, who is great and awesome, and fight for your brothers, your sons and your daughters, your wives and your homes'" (Nehemiah 4:13-14).

N ehemiah had received news about the dilapidated shape of Jerusalem's walls and that the gates had been burned down. He was distressed and wept upon hearing this news, and so he prayed to God.

He was cupbearer to the king, and when the king saw the sadness on his face, he asked him what was wrong. Again he prayed before answering the king. But then he asked King Artaxerxes to send him with men and supplies to rebuild the wall.

Nehemiah found favor from the Lord and was able to direct the rebuilding of the wall quickly, and had it built up to half of its entire height. Then the governor of nearby Samaria and some Ammonites heard of this and were going to attack Jerusalem to stop the building of the wall. So Nehemiah devised a great plan for how to guard against the oncoming attack. Again he led his men in prayer first. Then he thought that rather than just fighting to protect the wall, he should make it personal. In doing this, he gave the men a personal goal to fight for; the safety of their wives, sons, and daughters. Just as God called Nehemiah to rebuild the wall, he calls fathers and mothers to fight for each other and to fight for their children.

Certainly in marriage we all face times that are challenging, where we want to take the easy way out and give up. But what if we gave up in our business life each time we encountered a little resistance? God doesn't call us to be people who quit when things get tough, but to be overcomers.

We can all be overcomers if we draw on the strength of Jesus Christ, who is alive within us if we have a personal relationship with Him. We just need to dwell on what is at stake. God has strategically placed us as fathers or mothers, and we need to fight for each other and for our children.

For me, and for many fathers and mothers, there come heated times as parents when our children (usually as teenagers) will rebel against our authority. They will say things to us, which are hurtful and untrue. But what are we saying to them if we just give up — that they aren't worth fighting for? No.

Our children want us to be like Christ and show them unconditional love, regardless of the situation. They want to see us fight for their love, even if it isn't shining through to us at the particular situation we are in.

Our children, deep down, no matter what they say or do, know that we brought them into this world and that we have a special connection to them on all levels --spiritual, emotional, and physical.

If we give up on them, what does that say about what the rest of the world will do? Our children are watching our example to see what value we place on them, how far we are willing to go for them. Are you up to the challenge?

So continue to pursue a relationship with your children, no matter what they have done. Continue to show your unconditional love to them. Continue to show they matter to you. You will be amazed how God rewards you for your diligence and determination.

As fathers there is an additional responsibility we have, of fighting for our wives and to fight for family cohesiveness in times of division. We are the pursuers from the time before we are married, and it continues into our marriage. We have the responsibility to pursue our wives, and to never give up.

The Bible tells us to love our wives as Christ loved the church. And if we love them that deeply, we will go to any lengths to fight for them and fight for our children. So let us persevere and not grow weary, but fight in all occasions for our family.

16

2. Connect With Your Kids About School

As a first grade teacher, my wife Lisa is adept at drawing information out of children, although at this age their communication skills are limited. She is naturally gifted in communicating, especially with children.

She and I have discussed that there are different strategies or tactics which should be employed, not just with first grade children, but with children of all ages. Using the right phrases, questions, and attitude will get them to enjoy telling you about their day.

It can even become a game. At times in our family, our children knew the routine, and would run right through it after school before we would even prompt them. They would tell us the basic information, and then we would delve deeper into the "unchartered" territory. Strategies like this can dramatically open the communication channels throughout the entire family.

For example, if you say to your child when they enter the house after school, "How was school today?" you will limit your opportunities to learn much about what happened that day. That is because they can simply say, "Okay" or "Fine."

Contrast that with a probing question like, "What was the best thing and the worst thing that happened to you at school today?" Do you see the difference in the depth of the question and the corresponding answer?

Another example would be the question, "Do you like your teachers?" which leads to a yes or no answer. But if you present the question as, "Who do you think is your best teacher and why?" then the question demands an explanation.

So what you are seeking are more open-ended questions, where a dialogue can begin. Another question of this type is, "Who are your five best friends in school?" When this is answered, you can probe deeper by saying, "What is it you like most about (the friend they named best)?" You could even continue with, "What is it about the other friends that you like?"

These are a few ideas to get you started. But if you brainstorm, I'm sure you can come with other ways to make discussing school with your children an enjoyable, meaningful experience.

3. Eat Dinner Together (at Home)

I know there are many families that eat several of their meals out of the home each week. The majority of American families have both parents working and finding time to cook dinner and eat together around the dinner table is difficult. With children's extracurricular activities during the week, it makes eating dinner together at home even more difficult.

But there are rewards to taking the time to eat dinner together at home as a family. In fact, several Harvard research studies indicate the importance of eating dinner at home as a family. In *The Washington Post* a September 1981 article written by Anne Fishel indicates that the most important thing you can do with your children is to eat dinner with them.

In this article, Ms. Fishel (who is an associate clinical professor of Psychology at Harvard Medical School) states that among other things, dinner time conversation boosts vocabulary. This article also reported that family dinners result in more fruits, vegetables, vitamins and micro-nutrients being consumed. The research also indicated that regular family dinners lower the likelihood of drug use, binge drinking and other detrimental behaviors. I think the best thing about the research is it found that dinnertime was the time that children are most likely to talk to their parents.

Over the years my wife, Lisa, has done an excellent job of preparing dinners for our family. If you looked on our family calendars from ten years ago, you would find the main course that was planned for each day. The regular planned dinners placed a priority amongst our family members of coming together for a meal each evening.

Dinnertime was the time we would share our stories, our successes and our struggles with the entire family. The dinner table was the place that we prayed together and laughed together. It was a place we caught up on what each of us was doing in the family. Reflecting back on this time, I believe it was one of the times each day when the children's self-esteem

19

was heightened, because they had a voice at the table and could be praised or given encouragement.

Dinners around our kitchen table were given extra emphasis when we took in a young man from our community who was a friend of our daughter, Kaitlyn. He was 17-years old at the time and had a much larger appetite than our daughter's appetite.

So Lisa made a special effort to ensure dinners that he enjoyed were prepared each weekday evening. She even bought some new recipe books and implemented some new meals that were scheduled routinely on our calendars for the year and a half he lived with us.

I fondly look back on this time because having an additional person around the dinner table resulted in more lively conversation, and since now there was another male at the table, new dinner discussions evolved about sports, politics and other issues that were not previously big discussion topics in our house.

As I have discussed, the research indicates there are many reasons to gather together nightly around the dinner table. Perhaps that is one of the best things you can do as a family. For those that are more accustomed to eating out regularly, please remember that creative ways to eat as a family at home do exist. A great way to still have a dinner at home—even if there isn't time for cooking—is to leave something cooking in the crockpot all day.

In our family we have done this with pork roast, with ribs, with chili, and many types of soup. There are other meals that can be prepared that are not as elaborate such as paninis, or a fancy breakfast served at dinnertime or something prepared on the grill.

Other ideas can be found in books at grocery store checkout lines with titles like *Meals in Less than 30 Minutes* and the like. Based on the wealth of research on the topic indicating the multitude of benefits, investing time in cooking and eating at home is well worth the effort expended.

4. Bedtime Blessings

This nugget can be a blessing to your children that they will cherish for years to come. Several nuggets have already allured to the fact that quality time with your kids undoubtedly plays a big part in their development. Quality time with kids seems to shrink as they get older.

Daily life becomes busier and we parents must actively pursue windows of opportunity during the day when we can talk — really talk — with each child. In our family we found that one of those times is bedtime, and that bedtime was the best time to bond with younger children.

I think this is because there is no set agenda. We weren't sitting down for dinner. We weren't getting ready for school. We weren't heading out the door to go to an afterschool activity. Bedtime had no set ending time as each child (and sometimes the parent!) began to wind down to fall asleep.

Talking during this time was open-ended and, depending on their level of exhaustion we spent more or less time with them before we tucked them in to fall asleep. We have three children, who are three years apart in age. Because my wife and I looked forward to this time with each child, we would switch off—she would be with one child at bedtime, I would be with another. Then we would switch again so that we each spent twenty to thirty minutes with each child.

Now this was a huge time commitment for us, but we actually looked forward to it because of the closeness we developed with our children during this time. We would read books to them and pray with them. So bedtime became an ideal time for our kids to not only be open with us but for them to hear about our own childhood experiences.

Sometimes instead of reading books, the kids would ask us to tell a story. I remember telling our youngest child Megan (who was about six at the time) about a journey my brothers and I had made down a large creek when we were children.

On this trip we caught a bass fish, which was about twelve inches long. When I told this story to Megan, she would ask me how big the fish was, and I would tell her, "About this big…" and separate my hands about twelve inches.

She often asked me to retell the story, and every time she would repeat after me and say, "About this big…" and separate her hands about twelve inches apart. Then she would extend them as far as she could. She loved that story and she loved to interrupt me when we got to the point in the story where she asked how big the fish was. She is now 19, but will still mention the story occasionally when it is triggered in her mind. When this happens we just gaze into each other's eyes and fondly recall the fun we had with that story.

Another story that Megan modified during bedtime discussions involved a Christmas vacation trip to my Uncle's house near Detroit. This trip was memorable for me living in Atlanta, because it was like a winter land paradise when I arrived. There was fresh snow on the ground and the lake was frozen over to the extent my older cousin could drive his car on the lake. The lake always had ducks on it so I told Megan my story of how I ran up behind a duck and slid on my bottom and caught the duck between my legs.

My Uncle let me put it in the garage overnight and then we let it go the next day. But Megan would interrupt the story at the end during my telling of it and interject that "I put the duck in the freezer (instead of letting it go). I find it interesting that she would look forward to hearing the entirety of stories and then put her own twist on it to make it "her story" that she could conclude.

Another time I was talking with our daughter Ashley before she went to sleep and she asked me why I spent so much time talking about the Bible with her and praying with her at bedtime. I remember telling her that God always listens, He is always "on." He takes no breaks. So whenever we pray to Him, He hears our prayers. I told her that I knew I was saved and that I wanted to tell her Bible stories and pray with her so that she would grow in her own faith. I shared with her that I wanted more than anything for her to end up in heaven with me.

We often talked about heaven. A few years later, when Megan was about 8, our entire family gathered nightly to read aloud to the first three chapters of Don Piper's book *90 Minutes in Heaven.* Mr. Piper was in a horrific car accident and was pronounced dead at the scene. Yet ninety minutes later he miraculously awoke, singing a hymn. In his book, he tells of visiting heaven for those ninety minutes and describes the unimaginable beauty and the lovely music that was everywhere. His words portray heaven as majestic and royal as well as beautiful. We read the book for twenty or thirty minutes every evening for about a week or two which served to give them a mental vision of what heaven might be like when we get there. That special time yielded dividends when my Mom developed cancer and my wife and children would read to her from the book *Heaven is for Real*, by Todd Burpo and Lynn Vincent. I thank God for my wife and children doing that and believe our reading *90 Minutes in Heaven* in their younger years had a part in their hearts to share *Heaven is for Real* with my Mom as she was approaching death. What a blessing that was!

5. Find Opportunities to Affirm Your Kids

Recently my daughter Kaitlyn, who was living with us during her first year of teaching, was feeling a great deal of stress. This stress was brought on by the fact that she had started a new teaching position, stepping in during the middle of the school year for a teacher who had retired. So, while my daughter takes after my wife and is an excellent teacher and tutor, she was feeling overwhelmed by the amount of tests and subject matter the school system required her to cover before the end of the school year.

She was doing schoolwork in the evenings after school and after she completed her tutoring. But didn't feel she had adequate time to prepare all of her lesson plans and get all the grading done. It wasn't like she was not doing any schoolwork on the weekends. She would typically put in six to 10 hours of work on the weekend. But, although she felt behind, she had signed up for a women's small group in our church.

During this same time, my youngest daughter Megan was taking a challenging class load as a junior in high school, along with taking some challenging Advanced Placement courses, which counted toward her college credits. She also had other obligations after school, such as a leader in the Student Government Association and many other clubs that met after school.

On that same Tuesday night, she elected to go to the first meeting for high schoolers that our new 12 Stone Church satellite campus was having. I had hoped that she would be able to support the startup of this new group meeting within our local campus, and she made time in her schedule for this first meeting.

Oftentimes I will speak with my children about making time for something that is important to me or I feel is important to them. But this evening I had not lobbied for them to attend their respective church functions and I was very happy that they decided to take time out of their busy schedules for these church-related functions.

I spoke to each of them individually before bedtime to tell them why I thought this was important and how pleased I was that they had made the choice to put these activities before the other things demanding their attention. I told them that I wanted to show my affirmation of their decisions and would do so by doing something extra for them, to show them I thought they had made the right decision.

Since Chick-fil-A is my youngest daughter's favorite restaurant, I told her if she desired I would be at Chick-fil-A when they opened at 6:30 in the morning so that she could have a biscuit and still make it to school by 7:00 a.m. She quickly took me up on this offer! So I went to Kaitlyn and told her that I wanted to affirm her decision to trust God, and let her know that if she invested time in the small group, God would help her find a way to get everything done. I also mentioned to her that I was going to Chick-fil-A in the morning and would be happy to show my support of her decision by a buying a chicken biscuit for her. She liked the idea of this spontaneous reward for her decision and likewise said yes to my offer.

I certainly could do a better job of making these spontaneous gestures of support and affirmation, as they are not made nearly as frequently as they could or should be.

My point in this gold nugget is that I did reward my two daughters in this circumstance and they recognize the fact that this was something extra I was doing for them. They recognized that this was a reward they would not have received without making the decisions they did. And they recognized that I served them for their faithfulness to God.

The next morning, I woke up early and drove to Chick-fil-A and paid for their breakfast as a way to affirm their decisions. The best part of all is I received a grateful response from them and so it was a pleasure to serve them in this way.

6. Letters from Dad

As a father whose love language is words of affirmation I know there is tremendous power in writing down affirmation of other people and sharing it with them. I believe this is affirming to all, and that it is especially important to do this for our spouse, our children, and our parents.

Greg Vaughn is the author of the book, *Letters from Dad,* and president of a company founded to forward this concept. As members of a church we attended in the past, I and a group of fathers decided to go through a program of writing to our families.

We met several times together where we watched a DVD and worked through a workbook as part of this program. The program was designed to get dads involved in letter-writing campaigns to their families. Grace Products, the company Mr. Vaughn founded, sells copies of this workbook, which helps you prepare for writing to your wife and children and parents. I highly recommend the book and the workbook to help you prepare for a letter-writing campaign for your loved ones.

For those who do not feel that writing letters is one of your strengths, the workbook will be particularly helpful. This is because in addition to providing background on the subject the workbook includes a few example letters written to both wives, children, and parents which you can pattern your letters by.

In most of the letters I wrote to my family I found it useful to google what the recipient's name meant and include that in the letter near the beginning. Everyone likes to know what things mean and if you have never been told what the meaning of your name is it is a great way to create attention and provide insight into the person from the outset of the letter.

7. Let's Go Camping

When my wife and I were first married, cell phones had not even been unveiled onto the market. This was back in 1989, so there were less distractions in our life.

Texting was non-existent and the Internet was not used by the average person, if it was even available to the average person. Contrast that with today and how our cell phones are in some cases as powerful as our computers. They have built-in GPS, texting, and apps to do almost anything you can imagine now.

Not only do parents have cell phones today, but so do our children. With each advance in technology, our lives become busier and much more complex. Then the fact that you can communicate not only via text but via email, via Twitter, via Facebook or via Instagram really makes our life an "instant on" life.

My wife has seen the consequences of this in her classroom. Although she is not teaching upper grades but rather first grade in elementary school, she has observed that the average attention span of even her first graders has decreased.

She credits this to the fact that many of her first graders have tablets and computers and they spend considerable time on them playing games. This leaves less time to develop listening skills in their homes with their family.

I believe parents and their kids are spending a greater and greater percentage of their time on technology. What once was time spent reading books and discussing family matters is being squeezed out, and it is being reflected in the classrooms.

Think about your own children; how often do they look at their phone because of an incoming text or other form of communication? The general consensus is that our society is becoming more compartmentalized. That is because most parents and kids, even at a young age, have cell phones, and we are all wrapped up in our little world of friends and entertainment available on our phones.

We are spending less time as a family unit and more time by ourselves on the phone. If you look around at restaurants or shopping centers, or anywhere in public, you will see that for most people it will be less than five minutes before they check their phone. So, we are all caught up in this communication age where our attention is constantly diverted from what we were doing.

One rewarding activity my wife and I found which helps to combat the constant distractions is to go camping. Depending on where you go camping, there may not be a cell-phone signal for you to be connected to the outside world. But even if there is cell-phone coverage you can plan on a hiking excursion or other activity at the campground and make a conscious decision to leave all phones behind, except maybe one for emergency communications.

One of the places my wife and I liked to go camping the most with our children was deep in the mountains of North Georgia where there was no cell- phone coverage. These camping trips allowed us to take time to focus on things as a family.

Text messages from friends or boyfriends, or business phone calls disrupt the natural flow of things around our house. But in the mountains we could go putt-putt golfing without distraction, we could go out on the lake in a rowboat without distraction, and simple activities like roasting marshmallows around the campfire and singing camp songs united our family.

We established traditions on those camping trips that our children will reflect back on and hopefully carry on when they are older, married, and have children of their own. Both my wife and I had parents who took us camping, and so this is a family tradition that I hope kids pass on to the next generation.

I highly encourage you, even if you are not an outdoors person, to crawl out of your comfort zone and explore the wilderness of camping. It may be one of the best "growing experiences" you ever undertake.

8. Invent Games While On Vacation

Did your family play games while on vacation when you were a child? We used to play games in the car, like finding the letters to the alphabet on road signs, beginning with the letter A. I am sure your family had games you played while on vacation. This is something you and your siblings remember from when you were growing up.

One of the things that is great about vacations, is that you remember some incident or some tradition that was established while on vacation. These cause you to think back with fond memories on your family time. I encourage you to create traditions with your own children when on vacation, things you can all reflect back on and enjoy as you get older.

My wife and I established several traditions for vacations with our children. Vacation time, with no set schedule, is a great time to be creative and come up with games to entertain the family, which might even become a family tradition.

I remember two games that became part of the family vacation heritage. We traveled to Hilton Head Island when our oldest child was only one-year old. We enjoyed it so much that we made every effort to go to this same location every year after that. While we stayed in various vacation spots, we had the most fun staying in our camper in a campground on the island.

The camper was a full-sized travel trailer (8 feet high by 23 feet long). The campground we stayed at did not allow pop-up campers. It was a well-maintained campground, with large trees and manicured bushes distributed throughout it.

The streets in the campground were all paved, and since we had our bikes, we invented a game where we would play hide-and-seek on our bicycles. The campground was large enough, with many streets and bushes that were large enough to hide behind. So we had a great time and would look forward to riding around on our bikes playing rolling hide-and-seek each summer.

We also invented a game for the times we were just sitting around the picnic table. One of us would act out some aspect of a TV show, and all the others would try to guess the TV show. Whoever guessed the show would then get their chance at acting out a part and let the others guess what show it was.

So these were a couple of games we thought up or invented, in addition to the typical activities like going to the beach, getting ice cream, and other times that helped make our vacations memorable. I encourage you to give some thought to this on your next vacation and establish traditions for your family.

9. Give Thanks Around The Dinner Table

Our family has used many different prayers before dinner around our dinner table. If children are seated with us we will sometimes use a simple prayer that the children know. On other occasions one of our family members will offer to give a lengthier prayer. Additionally we have a few memorized short prayers which everyone has learned that we say together. But the one I want to emphasize in this gold nugget is one which glorifies God by thanking and praising Him. We employ this type of prayer, which was passed down from my wife's parents, once or twice a week. The practice in this prayer is to let each person seated around the dinner table state what you are grateful or thankful for.

We generally agree that we will all narrow what we are thankful for down to one item, although someone in the family will occasionally squeeze in a second item (not without some good natured ribbing from the rest of us). This is a neat way of sharing family information around the dinner table and learning what positive things occurred in each other's life that day, which can transition into further discussion after the prayer is concluded.

10. Unite Your Family

Particularly if you have younger children, this gold nugget could yield years of fun. It is based on the concept of treating someone in the family special and serving their needs by getting the other family members to join in their favorite activity.

It promotes harmony and unity in the family while also developing a respect or practice of submitting to others. I think that is important to develop in this world of "me first." As youngsters, it gives them the opportunity to learn that not everyone can be first simultaneously. It teaches them that there are times when you will be first and there are times when others must come first.

Before delving into this project it will be important to explain the thinking behind it to your children. Discuss with them that we want to celebrate with others at times like their birthdays and other milestones and as a group the way to do that is for the others to serve them for the greater good.

As a former soccer player I would say it is analogous to the soccer player, who doesn't have as good a shot at the goal as another player so he passes it to that player who scores the goal. The greater good is that the team scores a goal and so instead of taking the more difficult shot at the goal you pass it off for the greater good of the team.

This strategy of uniting your family comes about by having the whole family join in on one activity which one person chooses for that month. So, if one of your children's favorite activities is to go bowling, the whole family goes bowling to share that favorite activity.

The next month another child's desired activity is to go to a sports game. So the whole family does that activity one day that month. After each child has chosen a favorite activity, it's the mother's turn to choose what she wants to do for the next month. And finally, it's the father choice. Then the cycle starts over again and the first child can choose the same activity or a different one for the next time around.

You can also make a game out of it by adding the element of surprise. You could allow the one selecting the activity to announce the activity on the spur of the moment, rather than revealing it ahead of time. The important thing is that everyone wholeheartedly supports the person selecting the activity by submitting to their choice and making sure they have a good time—whether selected in advance or spontaneously.

You might need to improvise this basic strategy to fit your family's dynamic. Being creative with this basic theme of having fun together as a family is key—even if it isn't your personal favorite activity. The goal is to have fun and concurrently teach your children that even if the activity isn't something they really like doing, they will learn the life lesson that they must sacrifice sometimes and think of others.

11. Spread the Christmas Spirit

As Christians, Christmas is a day we look forward to and celebrate with friends and family. It can be a time when the hustle and bustle of decorating and shopping pushes Jesus out of the focal point and into the background.

Even on Christmas day for many the primary activity is on opening presents and eating a Christmas dinner together with family. Perhaps you find that consumerism and the obsession with buying gifts detract from the real meaning of Christmas. Turning our focus from ourselves to others, like Jesus did while on earth, may add to your joy on this special day. Activities that put others first that you can do on Christmas day require some creativity and initiative but can definitely heighten you Christmas experience.

Our family has been part of a group that has served the homeless in Atlanta in a small way on Christmas day. We joined a group of our friends who were already serving the homeless on Christmas Day about 9 years ago, and it has become a tradition in our family.

Our children, who are now young adults, find this activity one of their most cherished Christmas activities. This is true even though they must wake up at 6 AM to prepare for feeding the homeless breakfast on Christmas in downtown Atlanta.

It has grown to the point we now also give away gloves, lotion, toothbrushes, deodorant, and other staples. At one point our group had grown to over a hundred that would meet at a parking lot and then drive into Atlanta to feed the homeless. Now the numbers in our group are less but we still meet up with another group that gives away clothing that we met through feeding the homeless.

As a family we relish and look forward to starting our Christmas Day each year early in the morning serving others. It truly changes our outlook or disposition as we intermingle with the homeless and talk with them and encourage them. The expression "it is better to give than to receive" certainly applies to our Christmas morning experience.

After this experience coming home and opening gifts, while enjoyable, doesn't seem nearly as gratifying as meeting others at their time and place of need. It has become a family tradition that is intermingled with Christmas that we look forward to each year.

There are certainly other serving activities in every community, such as visiting a nursing center to go caroling or see patients who may not have family around. Perhaps you can think of other ways to serve others and spread the Christmas Spirit. Ho Ho Ho.

Gold Nuggets for Spiritual Growth

12. Are You Strong Enough To Surrender?

We found out my Mom had breast cancer that had progressed into her bones when she fell and broke her arm at age 84. After a month, it had not grown back together. The orthopedist ordered X-rays which indicated there was cancer at the site of the break which is why the bone would not grow together.

The doctor suggested surgery to install a titanium rod through the center of the humerus from the shoulder to the elbow. My Mom was weak and frail, having already lost weight from the cancer, and was only about 97 pounds.

Due to the cancer, she did not find food particularly appetizing and was not drinking adequate amounts of water, causing her to become dehydrated from time to time. But she had the surgery, and was released from the hospital. About two days later she was admitted into a nursing home where she began physical therapy to regain her strength and movement in her arm.

She verbalized to me that it was such an uphill battle that she didn't know if she was up for it. She was wavering in her ability to do everything that was required to get back to her independent apartment in the same retirement center. But her oncologist had said she had about an 80 % chance of regaining her health by taking the hormone pills which should stop the growth of the cancer in her body.

The day after my Mom told me that she didn't know if she could withstand the physical therapy nor eat enough to regain her strength, I was listening to a Christian music station. I heard a song, I believe for the first time. The song was "Strong Enough" by Matthew West.

The lyrics precisely fit the situation she was in — that she was not "strong enough" — that what she was going through looks like more than she could do on her own. This song touched me deeply and I asked my daughter, Kaitlyn, who was home from college, to take the lyrics printed on a piece of paper to her to read while Kaitlyn played the song from a CD on a portable CD player.

And I asked my Mom to agree to do three things, and to let the Lord take care of the rest. I asked her to eat as much as she could, to drink a lot of water daily, and to agree to push herself to do the required physical therapy daily. She agreed and amazingly she regained her strength. The hormone therapy worked and she also regained her taste for food. After a short time, she was able to move back into her independent apartment!

I tell you this story about my Mom and this song, because I asked her to do all she could, to surrender to God's will, and turn things over to Him. That is the essence of the song. At some point, we all face something that is bigger than we are — something that we cannot get through without God's help. Just as in my Mom's case, the key is to admit that we cannot do everything this world throws at us. But when we surrender to the Lord and place our trust in Him, He can do all things through us. In my Mom's case, she did that. She did surrender, and she did her part by doing all she could, and then she left the rest to God.

I had many good months with my Mom, but she did pass away about a year and a half later. Still there was an extra blessing that God showered us with on the day we held her Celebration of Life service. It brought me and my family great joy.

You see, my daughter Kaitlyn was in college, majoring in dance and math. She had been a member of a Christian dance company throughout high school and had performed many praise and worship dances. Before my Mom passed, we had asked Mom if she would allow Kaitlyn to dance to the song "Strong Enough" at her Celebration of Life service.

I watched with joy as my daughter performed the dance in the church, with the portable CD player playing the music, just as Kaitlyn had done to help her grandmother turn the corner in her recovery. Oh, what a joy it was to remember fondly the scenario in which my Mom was strong enough to surrender and let God work a wonder in her life. Thank you, Mom!

Below are the words to "Strong Enough" by Matthew West © 2010 Songs of the Southside Independent Music Publishing.

"Strong Enough"

You must
You must think I'm strong
To give me what I'm going through

Well, forgive me
Forgive me if I'm wrong
But this looks like more than I can do
On my own

I know I'm not strong enough to be
Everything that I'm supposed to be
I give up
I'm not strong enough
Hands of mercy won't you cover me
Lord right now I'm asking you to be
Strong enough
Strong enough
For the both of us

Well, maybe
Maybe that's the point
To reach the point of giving up

Cause when I'm finally
Finally at rock bottom
Well, that's when I start looking up
And reaching out

I know I'm not strong enough to be
Everything that I'm supposed to be
I give up
I'm not strong enough
Hands of mercy won't you cover me

Lord right now I'm asking you to be
Strong enough
Strong enough

Cause I'm broken
Down to nothing
But I'm still holding on to the one thing
You are God
And you are strong
When I am weak

I can do all things
Through Christ who gives me strength
And I don't have to be
Strong enough
Strong enough

I can do all things
Through Christ who gives me strength
And I don't have to be
Strong enough

Strong enough
Oh, yeah
I know I'm not strong enough to be
Everything that I'm supposed to be
I give up
I'm not strong enough
Hands of mercy won't you cover me
Lord right now I'm asking you to be
Strong enough
Strong enough
Strong enough[1]

---

1. Used By Permission of ALFRED MUSIC.

13. Forgiveness

> You have heard that it was said to people long ago, "Do not murder, and anyone who murders will be subject to judgment." But I tell you that anyone who is angry with his brother will be subject to judgment... ...Therefore, if you are offering your gift at the altar and there remember that your brother has something against you, leave your gift there in front of the altar. First go and be reconciled to your brother; then come and offer your gift. (Matthew 5:21, 23, 24 - From Jesus' Sermon on the Mount)

In biblical times, the Jewish believers publicly brought their financial offerings to the temple. This is one of the highest forms of worshiping God, to honor him with tithes and gifts. Yet in this passage, Jesus, is conveying that even worshipping God by bringing him our offerings is less important than restoring broken fellowships with those around us.

Opportunities to offend and be offended abound in life, so the mechanics of repentance and forgiveness are foundational to healthy living. Without this reconciliation we tend to harden our hearts and put up walls between us.

This gives a foothold to the enemy, just like Pharaoh did when he hardened his heart. And with time, through continuing to harden his heart, Pharaoh lost his son. If forgiveness has become nearly impossible to you in some area, then asking Jesus for help is the first step.

At the core of our hearts, we want our desires to include coming alongside others, building them up, loving them. By doing so we are spreading the kingdom of God.

Matthew West's song "Forgiveness" says it well. The lines read:

> It flies in the face of all your pride
> It moves away the mad inside
> It's always anger's own worst enemy

Even when the jury and the judge
Say you've got a right to hold a grudge
It's the whisper in your ear saying, "Set it free"
Forgiveness, forgiveness

It'll clear the bitterness away
It can even set a prisoner free
There is no end to what its power can do
So, let it go and be amazed
By what you see through eyes of grace
The prisoner that it really frees is you
Forgiveness, forgiveness.[2]

I especially like the line "it's the whisper in your ear." Often I will sense what to do in a situation if I am simply willing to listen to that still, small inner voice that lines up with the Holy Spirit. And "the prisoner that it really frees is you," really hits the nail on the head.

Withholding forgiveness always hurts the one offended more than the offender. We actually hurt ourselves more than the one with whom we are angry; we never win. We would do well to ask God's help to forgive those that hurt us, to heed the scripture from Colossians 3:13 "Bear with each other and forgive whatever grievances you may have against one another. Forgive as the Lord forgave you."

_____

2. 2010 Songs of the Southside Independent Music Publishing, All Rights Reserved, Used by Permission of ALFRED MUSIC

14. Love Makes the World Go 'Round

"'Teacher, which is the greatest commandment in the Law?' Jesus replied: 'Love the Lord your God with all your heart and with all your soul and with all your mind.' This is the first and greatest commandment. And the second is like it: 'Love your neighbor as yourself.' All the Law and the Prophets hang on these two commandments" (Matthew 22: 36-40).

This gold nugget should be especially enjoyable to all those who love math. I was strong in math and as an engineer took many courses in calculus in college, in addition to geometry, algebra, and trigonometry in high school.

While working on the writing for this book God brought a verse to mind. I began recording the thoughts that came to mind regarding scriptures leading to the title of this nugget. What flowed out onto the paper was proof in verbal language similar to what would be done in geometry proving the correlation of angles in a triangle or parallelogram.

There is a lot packed away in this passage from Matthew. Referring to my Life Application Bible a note for this passage reads: "By fulfilling these two commands, a person keeps all the others." Then it goes on to say, "Jesus says that if we truly love God and our neighbor, we will naturally keep the (all the) commandments."

That is a powerful statement, which seems reasonable to me. We know that God is love. The apostle John confirmed this in 1st John 4:8 when he wrote: "Whoever does not love does not know God, because God is love."

Therefore, if God is love, and God makes the world (earth) go around because He created it that way, thus the statement, Love makes the world go 'round. Yes where would we be without God's love? God sacrificed his Son for us, Jesus Christ, because He loved us so much, He wants us to enjoy life to the full and then join Him in Heaven.

God wants us to be restored with Him like it was before the fall of Adam and Eve. He created Adam and Eve in his image, and He desires for us to be pure like He is, He desires the best for us. God loves us so much that although we are not pure, although we sin over and over, He still forgives us when we ask it of Him in prayer. Yes, God is love, and what a rich, deep love it is; a perfect love for each of us regardless of what we do, He still loves us the same. It is no wonder that Jesus stated as it is recorded in 1st Corinthians 13:13; "And now these three remain: faith, hope and love. But the greatest of these is love." Yes love does make the world go 'round.

15. Gratitude

In 2003, I went to Honduras on a mission trip with a group from the Methodist church that our family attended. I had never been on a mission trip before but my brother Ron, who was single at the time had been on five or six different trips.

He was interested in going with our group and offered to pay my way. I was thankful for his generosity and grateful he wanted to go. He and I were the closest in age of all of my brothers and had done many things together in our younger years. This trip would offer us the opportunity to spend a week together as adults working together in a spiritual setting.

The trip was a bonding experience as my brother and I roomed together in the hotel and rode together in the van from the hotel to the church where we worked. In the evenings, the group would gather around the hotel pool and tell the high points of the day. Much of what was shared really touched our hearts, and we felt the Holy Spirit at work.

God worked especially worked on my heart during this trip as I developed a strong sense of gratitude. I became aware of our family's blessings in contrast to the poverty of the village where we were building a church.

It was hard to think of our house, decorated with nice furniture and accessories in contrast to the fact that most of these families had few, if any, personal belongings. The fact was many of the families lived in shacks.

One family I particularly remember lived adjacent to a field where we would play soccer with the townspeople. The family's home was composed of cardboard, thin plastic, and corrugated sheet metal randomly put together. This shack-like structure was probably only eight feet by ten feet in size and had a dirt floor. Six family members lived in it. In my mind, the well-decorated house I lived in stood in stark contrast to this poor, decrepit shack and the reality of this really tugged on my heart.

It gave me a new sense of gratitude for all that we take for granted in the US and a new attitude that I would be fine no matter what the future held, for I had more than I needed anyway. But it also filled my heart with respect for the strength and determination these humble families had.

I acquired a sense of gratitude on this trip that heretofore was non-existent living in our Atlanta suburb. In Atlanta, my mind had been sheltered from the realities of the depraved conditions that most people in third world countries experience.

It had not even crossed my mind; I was just caught up on the run mill of life, like a hamster spinning around trying to keep up with the Jones or Smiths. Then this trip made me stop, consider the plight of others and decide what to do moving forward from this encounter with poverty.

Through possibly not a conscious decision, but rather a spiritual awakening, I began to be grateful for so many of the things that I had taken for granted previously. I believe that this newfound gratitude developed in me a more generous and giving spirit for I believed that I already possessed everything I needed in life, just not everything I wanted.

That desire for more was just propagated by this American culture we live in. It shifted my thinking from, "I need to work harder so I can obtain this" to one of gratitude and being blessed for what God has given to me. I also thank Him for this attitude adjustment and for the blessing of this mission trip and showed me how I can use what He has given me to give to those who have far less. I think He would desire for us not to be dissatisfied with what we don't have, but to be grateful for what we do have and to give to others because He has given to us.

16. Worship with Praise and Conviction

Have you ever had a friend who bought a house and later you took them a housewarming gift? The housewarming gift was a way to celebrate a significant milestone with them and to show your love for them. You were rejoicing with them that after their searching and finding a house (and then negotiating for the purchase), this was something to celebrate!

I believe we, in the same way, should bring our celebration and praise into God's house each time we come for worship. He does great things for us and it is only right and fitting that we worship Him with our heart and soul when we walk through the doors of His house of worship.

Churches begin services with a time of worship to praise and honor Him for what He has already done. We enter with joy and offer Him the gift of our music, voices, and words as we celebrate with one another in a corporate setting what God is doing in and around us.

Just think how pleasing it must be to God when so many likeminded Christians come into church and simultaneously offer up all we have in worship to glorify our God and King. If God meets two or three when they come together (Matthew 18:20 – "For where two or three come together in my name, there am I with them"), how much more must He meet us and join in celebrating when we come together for corporate worship as we praise Him and thank Him.

God makes it abundantly clear to us in His Word that we should praise Him in worship and how we should go about it. One of my favorites is Psalm 100:1-4, "Shout for joy to the Lord, all the earth. Worship the Lord with gladness; come before him with joyful songs. Know that the Lord is God. It is he who made us, and we are his; we are his people, the sheep of his pasture. Enter his gates with thanksgiving and his courts with praise; give thanks to him and praise his name."

The message that comes across to me here is that as we enter the doors of the church, we should be focused on Jesus and the joy that we have through Him. And don't you know Satan loves to distract us from achieving what it says here in Psalm 100.

I find it no wonder that many are late to church and miss out on one or more of the hymns or songs. It does not surprise me that siblings argue or fight in the car on the way to church. The enemy wants to thwart our plans to come together with joy in a corporate setting.

I have sensed this often, especially before Christmas and Easter services. Knowing the spiritual battle that undoubtedly is taking place in the spiritual realms, we are wise to plan ahead on how to circumvent the Enemy's plans.

Some actions we can take to accomplish this is to get up a half hour earlier on Sundays to arrive at church and be seated five minutes before the service. Perhaps another step you could take weekly or several times a month that would help establish a joyous, optimistic atmosphere for children is to treat them to something special for breakfast, like Krispy Kreme donuts! (While sugar-laden food before church with young children might not be the best of ideas, this is one practice my parents employed that always led to eager anticipation for our Sunday mornings.)

A final tactic to assist in your Sunday morning routine is to talk with your children about Psalm 100—not on Sunday morning when it is hectic, but on Saturday night or in your devotion time during the week.

Explain to them why we come with a joyous heart (verse 3 of Psalm 100) and how we should enter, think, and worship as we come each week. It may be beneficial to explain to your children that we are joyous on Easter Sunday because we are celebrating Jesus' ascension from the grave.

Continue explaining that each Sunday we should likewise be joyous because we are entering the house that Jesus built, and how that is the one time we join with other believers and celebrate all that God is doing in our lives. For our God is a good, good Father and He yearns to hear our praise and adoration.

17. Aspire Authority in Heaven

Then the mother of Zebedee's sons came to Jesus with her sons and, kneeling down, asked a favor of him. "What is it you want?" he asked.

She said, "Grant that one of these two sons of mine may sit at your right and the other at your left in your kingdom." "You don't know what you are asking," Jesus said to them. "Can you drink the cup I am going to drink?" "We can" they answered. Jesus said to them, "You will indeed drink from my cup, but to sit at my right or left is not for me to grant. These places belong to those for whom they have been prepared by my Father." (Matthew 20:20-23)

Jesus does not tell this mother that there is not a hierarchy in Heaven. On the contrary, He confirms there is a hierarchy in heaven but that it has been established by His Father in Heaven. I find it puzzling that most people (and even most Christians) strive hard for promotions and upward mobility in the workplace, yet seemingly they are unaware that there is a hierarchy in heaven.

I credit this to the fact that most people are unknowledgeable about things of Heaven, and even a bit naive. Otherwise, it would seem foolish to focus on hierarchy, workplace positions, and compensation here on earth—where at most there are 40 or 50 years of rewards—versus the rewards in heaven, which go on for eternity.

Knowing this, where would you put your efforts? Do you focus on earthly gain and recognition or on heavenly gain and authority? If Christians really studied God's Word and investigated what it says about Heaven, there should be a mass rush or revival by Christians—with a mindset on achieving the highest positions of power in Heaven.

Another Scripture which informs us there are authorities in heaven is 1 Peter 3:22 where it is written: "[Jesus Christ,] who has gone into heaven and is at God's right hand- with angels, authorities and powers in submission to him." Here we read that there are authorities and powers in heaven, and they are in submission to Jesus.

Also in Revelation 21:24, the Bible speaks of the new heaven and new earth in these words, "The nations will walk by its light, and the kings of the earth will bring their splendor into it."

By these words we see that there will be other nations, not just a New Jerusalem on the New Earth, and Kings also. So there will be many positions and authorities that those who go to heaven will assume in the New Heaven and New Earth. An excellent biblical resource on this—in addition to going directly to the Bible—is in the book *The Real Heaven*, by Chip Ingram.

In his book, Ingram writes, "Our roles in heaven will be determined by Jesus, according to how we lived on this earth. God gave to each of us a certain amount of time and treasure and talent. How we steward our lives here will determine our reward and our role in heaven."

Let this sink into your soul. We are responsible for how we live on earth. And how we live on earth determines our place in heaven. May we each realize the weight of these words and live on earth with a focus on Heaven.

18. Let Love Abound

As I write and approach the completion of this book, there have been recent police shootings of African Americans in various cities throughout America. These shootings, and shootings of policemen, along with protests by athletes during the National Anthem before football games, have raised tensions in America. There appears to be more racial tension than at any time during recent history.

My expectation is the tension will escalate and there will be more incidents with higher numbers of people getting killed or shot. My hope is that people will turn to God for answers, and that love will make a way, that love will abound. That love for one another will be rekindled through Jesus Christ. That we will realize that every life matters, whether black, white, Hispanic, or Asian—every life matters to God, and should matter to us.

God created us in His image. He loves us perfectly as only our heavenly Father can do. Because of His love for us, He desires that "none should perish." This is stated in 2nd Peter 3:9 "The Lord is not slow in keeping his promise, as some understand slowness. He is patient with you, not wanting anyone to perish, but everyone to come to repentance."

Although the Lord knows each of our flaws, He looks at who we can be, what we will become if we repent and surrender our heart to Him. He sees us as we will be in heaven—pure and holy—instead of adulterated and sinful as we are until we are transformed into His likeness.

God loves us perfectly and it is through faith in Jesus Christ that we can aspire to that type of love where we love others more than ourselves. When we focus our eyes on God, and not the world, we can look at others with a heart of love, as God does, always wanting their best.

Depending on which version of the Bible you read, the Bible uses the word love about 500 times. I think it is significant that Paul, writing in 1 Corinthians 12 and after talking about the spiritual gifts God gives, he mentions love before moving to the 13th chapter on love. He includes the topic of love in the last sentence stating, "And now I will show you the most excellent way" (1 Corinthians 12:31).

The most excellent way Paul is referring to here is love. My Bible application on my phone precedes that last sentence with the heading, "Love Is Indispensable." Yes, without love I don't think the racial tension in our country will be resolved. But if you listen to the words of 1 Corinthians 13, you can imagine how love could break through and heal and restore.

Paul uses powerful words in verses 5 through 7, "It is not rude, it is not self-seeking, it is not easily angered, it keeps no record of wrongs. 6 Love does not delight in evil but rejoices with the truth. It always protects, always trusts, always hopes, always perseveres."

I believe there is an evil spirit of offense that is hovering over the United States. It is affecting many aspects of life in the U.S.—including racial tension. I believe the spirit of love conquers all, and if we turn to God in prayer on this issue, that He will lead us out of this conflict.

Suggested Prayer:

Father, the struggles our nation is facing trouble us greatly. I ask Father, in the name of Jesus, that You would intercede for our nation. Where there is division, bring unity. Where there is sorrow, bring healing. Where there is animosity, bring compassion and reconciliation. Where there is hatred, bring love. Father, You are bigger than any problem facing us individually, or any problem facing our country at large. We pray that in the spiritual realms You would send Your spiritual forces to defeat and eliminate any evil spirit of offense over our country and that Your spirit of love would pour out over all Americans as a spirit of love and a spirit of revival. Thank You, Father, that You love each of us, and desire that no one should perish. We desire that there be unity and love rather than the discord or racial tension. In the midst of so much hostility, may You bring many to know Jesus as their personal Savior and cover our nation with Your healing grace. Amen.

Gold Nuggets for a More Fulfilling Marriage

19. Know Your Spouse's Love Language

About ten years ago in a Sunday school class, my wife Lisa and I were exposed to the book, *The Five Love Languages* by Gary Chapman, first published in 1995 by Northfield Publishing. Mr. Chapman describes five ways to express and experience love in what he calls "love languages."

He describes five ways to express and experience love:

- Words of affirmation
- Quality time
- Receiving gifts
- Acts of service
- Physical touch

He explains that your chosen love language is the method that you would most like to receive love from your significant other.

After first going through this exercise with my wife, we learned that her love language was acts of service and mine was words of affirmation. Lisa would most appreciate or feel the most loved when I did acts that would take one task off her "to do list", or when I would do something that served her. For myself, I most appreciated and desired for Lisa to affirm me by verbally expressing words of affirmation. This might be through a comment like, "You did a good job fixing that broken water pipe." Or, "You did a great job of presenting your lesson to the Sunday school class today." While these examples sound like easy things to do, they actually are quite difficult. Why? Because we each operate from the love language we most desire to be expressed to us. So, thinking and acting outside of our own love language seems foreign to us. Learning to speak a different love language (i.e. the love language of our spouse) is like learning a foreign language; it's totally new to us. We have to learn to use a different part of our brain, not the one we are most comfortable with. So this takes some time and practice to speak a different love language effortlessly, without thinking. I must admit, at first I didn't do a very good job. It required time to think about her needs and what she would like. It seemed I was more occupied with what I wanted and the needs of the children. But God is a good God, and in the fall of 2015 God gave me a second opportunity to "get it right." I often attended a church service by myself on Wednesday nights where the primary emphasis was on healing. One Wednesday night, the exercise was to learn you and your spouse's love language. I half-heartedly went through the exercise, thinking I already knew this information. It was enjoyable to hear all the comments from the other attendees that night about learning their own love language or their spouses' love language. God would soon use this exercise to bring about a profound change in my life.

On the way home from the church, I started thinking again about Lisa's love language being acts of service. I knew I really loved my wife, but if she didn't feel my love to the same extent that I felt it towards her, that was my fault. I must not be "speaking" her love language enough. As I was driving, the conviction of the Holy Spirit came upon me, and I was so remorseful for having let my wife down that I starting weeping. I was weeping so intensely I almost had to pull off of the road because my eyes were filled with water from the tears. I repented on the spot and told God I was sorry for not loving my wife like Jesus loved the Church— like it tells us to do in Ephesians. I told God I was sorry for not putting Lisa's needs above my own. God convicted me that while I did a great job of loving strangers and putting God first, I needed to demonstrate to Lisa that I loved her above all things—other than God. I told Him that I was sorry. Now I needed to convince Lisa of just how much I loved her. I needed to ask her to forgive me for loving her the way I wanted to love her, instead of expressing my love to her—through HER love language of acts of service. When I arrived at my house I briefly told Lisa about my experience in the car, and that I was going to make changes. The next morning as we were both in the bathroom getting ready for work, I committed to her how much I did love her and that I was going to express my love through acts of service.

Prior to this experience, I did not assist my wife each morning in getting out the door for her teaching job. She would feed the dog. She would make her coffee (since I do not drink coffee). She would make her smoothie each morning. She would get her lunch out of the fridge, and then she would gather together her papers for school that day. I made the decision and told Lisa that each morning I was going to get up early and make her smoothie, fix her coffee, and feed the dog. I do that every weekday now and I also started showing her that she was first—even when it came to church meetings. I began to ask her if she was OK with me going to these extra services, rather than just telling her that was what I was going to do. (All the while, I thought I was doing the right thing by putting God first.) In His grace, God showed me that communicating with your wife to see if there is some special situation she is dealing with is more important than being at every religious event I want to go to.

It was amazing to see God work in our relationship as a result of the conviction He had placed on me. Almost immediately, Lisa's attitude towards me changed. She was much more pleasant and welcoming. I can imagine that before she thought, "Oh here is my husband appearing so spiritual, but he doesn't think of me before himself and doesn't help me out in the mornings." But after I made this change I could perceive that she now regarded me as her partner—to assist her and be a blessing to her. About nine days after God convicted me of my need for change, I wrote in my journal that Lisa told me she could see a difference already in my putting her first.

To summarize this gold nugget, I would say you not only have to know your spouse's love language, you need to put that knowledge into practice. Even if you know you love your spouse like I did my wife, you must express it in their love language so they feel your love being extended to them. You will you have spoken her love language when your spouse tells you, "Yes, I know you love me because of this or that . . . something specific they can identify that you do for them.

So, if their love language is touch, touch your spouse often in ways to let them know you are thinking of them. If their love language is receiving gifts, give gifts to them regularly and often. They don't have to be expensive gifts; they will appreciate your thoughtfulness in coming up with clever gifts to give them. If their love language is quality time, look for chunks of time you can devote to him or her. Ask them what they would like to do on the weekend or whenever that chunk of time is. It all comes down to thinking of your spouse before yourself. Put your mind in their love language mindset so they will appreciate and value your efforts.

20. Be a Non-Anxious Presence

As husbands, there are many ways that we can support our wives and love them as Jesus loved the church as Paul directed in the book of Ephesians. I believe one of the best ways to support our wives is to be a calming force in their lives. That would take on many facets in the life of a couple and so there are many opportunities for the husband to be a blessing to his wife—with his calming presence.

An example would be when a situation becomes tense between a husband and wife, and a disagreement or argument ensues. The husband should take the lead role in being the one to live this down. The husband should be the one not to raise his voice, and he should do his part not to elevate a discussion into a heated argument.

Not that this is easy to do and not that I have done a great job of this, particularly before submitting my life to Jesus. But in submitting my life to Jesus, am I not in essence stating that I am living for Him—to do what would bring Him glory? So, I have grown in my role as a husband as God has shown me that as the head of the household I'm responsible for maintaining the civility in my relationship with my wife.

I understand His purpose is served better in our marriage if instead of a discussion elevating to a shouting match that I learn to listen and say nothing. Or better yet, submit to my wife and her viewpoint on the occasions when she feels strongly about something.

Wouldn't God's purposes be better served if I try to see her side and meet her more than 50 percent of the way? Again, it has taken me many years to see this clearly in my relationship with Lisa, but now I can execute this practice in our life at a much greater percentage of the time.

When we were going through the most difficult years of our marriage, a marriage counselor told me in front of Lisa that he thought I needed to do everything that she wanted me to do for the next year in our relationship. This goes against everything you are taught in this world.

This world tells you that everything should be fair, so I believed that everything in a marriage should be 50% the will of the husband and 50% the will of the wife. So here was this counselor telling me that our relationship should be entirely determined by her wishes! Obviously, I had a hard time seeing his point of view and so I sought the advice of a group of men, who were meeting with me and assisting me as Lisa and I navigated this difficult time in our marriage.

It wasn't practical for me to concede to her every desire, but I came to realize that I had hurt Lisa over the years and in order to restore her trust in me, I had to do the lion's share of the rebuilding work. So for a season the relationship became more like 80% her will or desires to 20% my desires. God worked on my heart and I was able to see her point of view on more things, but it still took many years after this for me to consistently avoid (or not escalate) heated discussions.

I have heard this before in sermons but recently heard from Pastor Kevin Queen of Cross Point Church. He said one of the roles of the Holy Spirit is to counsel, and he went on to say that one of the greatest gifts of a counselor is a non-anxious presence.

As one who has been the party to many counseling sessions, that resonates with me. Who would want to meet with a counselor who was on edge and anxious, who did not let you finish your sentences before interrupting you, or who raised his voice to you during counseling. Since hearing this, I have realized that this is true for husbands also.

It's no wonder Lisa was frustrated by me when I always sought to win any discussion that elevated into an argument. As an aggressive Type A personality I was more than willing to argue my point until I "won." But now I see the greater good, and the approach that brings glory to God is for me to be calm, to never elevate the discussion and to be her friend instead of her opponent.

That knowledge gives me much foresight when an issue does come up. I now strive to be a non-anxious presence that will result in Lisa being more willing to open up to me about anything, because she knows I won't always try to steer her to my thinking or convince her I am right. I am not perfect at accomplishing this, but my batting average is much higher. Lisa is much more relaxed and more like her natural self around me now, rather than being guarded and reserved. As a result my non-anxious presence is a blessing to our relationship. I know what the goal is in every discussion I have with her and even if I don't achieve it every time, it is helpful to know what I should do.

21. Do Something Unique for Your Wife

We know that all women like to be romanced, and one of the things that makes a romantic gesture memorable is if it is unique. Therefore, the element of surprise plays a large role in determining the overall romantic factor.

This seems to be all the craze in high school now with the creative ways boys ask girls to the Prom. I believe we should continue that element of surprise into marriage lest our marriages become dull and boring.

So how do we accomplish that? I believe that time reflecting and praying on the issue will yield a bounty of creative solutions that will keep the element of surprise alive in our marriages.

When we do that for our wives, they are more inclined to reciprocate with various gestures that will contribute to a more fulfilling marriage. One way might be to take your wife out on a dramatic date, which typically would be reserved for the weekend, on a weeknight.

Additionally, keeping the date a secret until the last moment always adds an element of surprise. This is exactly what I did about four years ago, not just for a date, but for a weekend anniversary trip. I made all the plans for our anniversary but told my wife that the destination would remain a secret. I knew she had always wanted to go to the Biltmore House in Asheville, North Carolina.

So I planned a trip, along with a route that would keep her from guessing our destination until we were about 20 minutes away. Throughout the ride, we had several nice conversations talking about where I might be taking her. Her anticipation as well as the conversations that followed made for a great start to a very memorable anniversary.

A Valentine's weekday date to Atlanta also brings about the same fond memories of out-of-the-ordinary romance early in our marriage. While Lisa was working as an elementary school teacher, she had a very good relationship with her principal and as a result, I had become friends with this principal.

I called the principal at school and told her I would like to take Lisa to a hotel after work on the night before Valentine's Day, and asked her if she could arrange a substitute teacher for Lisa on Valentine's Day.

Then I had roses delivered to the school on February 13th. At the end of the day Lisa went up to the office and was greeted with the roses and was told by the principal that she was scheduled off on Valentine's Day, which really caught her off guard.

However, she still didn't know what I had arranged until she arrived home and I told her I had taken a day of vacation and that I had booked a Valentine's package at a local hotel that night, including champagne and chocolates!

Being a teacher who was getting a day off during the week this went over in a big way with her, and the hotel package was very nice. This spontaneous and surprising evening made for a memory on Valentine's Day that neither she nor I would forget.

I hope these examples stir you to think creatively and see how the element of surprise can add to the romanticism of the moment at all ages.

22. Never Go to Sleep Mad

One of the best pieces of advice Lisa and I ever received was given to us by the pastor, who married us in 1989. He had given us each psychological testing to indicate what we were like individually, what philosophies we agreed on, and the areas where we were different—where problems might develop.

We were required to meet with the pastor several times prior to our marriage. During one of these pre-marital meetings, he shared that a key to his and his wife's marriage was that they agreed to never go to sleep mad at one another. If some disagreement developed, he said they agreed to talk through the problem and then kiss and makeup before turning the lights off.

My wife and I both agree that starting each day with a clean slate—not carrying over into the morning any disagreements or arguments from the previous day— is paramount. We made a practice of kissing and making up, before going to sleep.

Notice the word used was sleep rather than bed. There have been many times when we have been busy and not found time during the day to discuss an issue that we disagreed about, but we resolved ahead of time that we would settle our differences before we fell asleep.

This practice in a marriage is the key to keeping open communication. That meant if something was unresolved before bedtime, we would discuss the issue in bed with the expected outcome of resolving it before going to sleep.

The psychology employed here is that disagreements are inevitable, so having a strategy where the expected outcome is that the disagreement will be resolved before the end of the night points you towards that goal. That creates an environment where you are working together to accomplish the same thing before an issue even develops. You have already decided to be in agreement—pre-conflict—that all disagreements should be resolved prior to sleep, so that they do not carry over to the next day.

23. Bulletproof Your Marriage

It is a widely recognized fact that both Christian marriages and non-Christian marriages alike have about the same divorce rate of 50%. We know that God hates divorce, but we also know that God is a loving God who forgives us of our sins and that we are not defined by divorce or mistakes that we make in life.

We were created by God and for God. So while our relationship with our spouse is important, we exist primarily to be in relationship with God. God wants to bless our marriages and us. Family Life Today conducted a survey that indicated that only 8 percent of the couples prayed together.[3]

The survey also found that only one percent of the couples that prayed together had marriages end in divorce. So this seems to be the magic bullet, the bullet that might change the landscape in your marriage and in others. Because most couples' schedules start at different times in the morning and are busy with work during the day, a good time to come together and prayed together is at in the evening.

An opportune time for husbands and wives to pray together if their children are at an age to be left alone may be directly after dinner, and perhaps have the children cleaning the dishes. If the children are younger another strategy would be to wait until lying in bed to say a prayer together, which is a great way to end the day.

Whether Christian or not all couples face challenges in their marriage. Finding time for prayer time together, in addition to daily devotion time, is one strategy which according to this study will pay dividends for all couples. I pray it is one you will make time for in your daily lives.

---

3. I wish to credit Pastor Kevin Queen, who presented a teaching in 12 Stone Church on February 15, 2015, which included reference to a Family Life Today study. This study cited the statistics of Christians who pray together as a couple and the divorce rate for them.

24. Weekend Retreats with Your Spouse

In the early years of our marriage, my wife and I attended an in-town Atlanta church, and were members of a Sunday school class with many parents with young children. This was before I had started my home inspection business, but one of the other members of the class, who was a church leader, owned an electrical contracting company. As we became better friends, he shared with me one of his practices which I would like to pass along to you.

He and his wife would plan weekend retreats to the beach or to the mountains. The retreats would be taken "without children and with the purpose of planning for their family's future, particularly their children's. They would discuss their business plans also on these trips, to include business goals and schedules, but the primary emphasis was schedules, plans, and goals for their children.

Most couples like to get away for a short weekend trip like this. But this is an excellent way to take time to be together and also take a little bit of a business approach to running the family. Time away provides emotional margin so couples can make formal plans and goals that they agree on. Just as in any business, goal setting helps you end up attaining the goals you are striving to reach.

Make sure you take time to write these goals down with a start and proposed finish date. Also make note of specific responsibilities or tasks you or your wife have to accomplish these goals. Goal setting can be fun while helping you set a strategic course for your family's future.

25. My Best Move for My Family

There are many different ways to fight for what God wants in your family. I want to talk in this gold nugget about what was my best decision in my ongoing fight for my family.

In December 2003, I was on a business trip, returning to Atlanta from an overnight stay in South Georgia. My wife and I had been seeing a marriage counselor. Yet I didn't feel that we were resolving the difficulties in our marriage. I had become frustrated that, no matter how hard I tried, there still seemed to be a great divide in our marriage. I was faithfully going to church and reading the Bible and felt a desire to grow spirituality.

My wife had shared with me that a Christian radio station had begun broadcasting in Atlanta, and I found myself switching from listening to rock 'n' roll stations to this Christian FM radio station. I also had started listening to a Christian AM radio station, which would re-broadcast a few pastors' sermons. Earlier that year in March, I had gone on my first mission trip to Honduras with my brother Ron, and about 12 other members from my church.

Through these activities, I felt an ongoing desire to get even closer to God and to have a deeper relationship with the Lord. I remember on two different occasions in 2003 watching TV and having a salvation call extended by the pastor or whoever was giving the message. I also remember saying, I want to say "yes" to Jesus Christ. I want Him to come into my life and be my personal Savior," but there was no commitment, no change in my heart.

But on a return trip to Atlanta in December of 2003 all that changed. I was listening to a Focus on the Family cassette tape entitled "Praying for Your Family," by Jack Hayford. While driving on Interstate 75 listening to this sermon, I found myself saying, "I am trying to do all of these things on my own to make my marriage better but none of that is working."

One of the things I had done earlier that year was to sell a prized possession — a 1987 Camaro IROC-Z. You see, I had paid cash for that car in 1987 before I even met my wife. I drove it hard when I drove it and had done some SCCA autocross racing in it. I had won the Atlanta chapter of SCCA for my division of cars for two years.

I also had driven the car to Salina, Kansas, for the national championship in my division of cars (where I found I was badly outclassed). I took a lot of pride in the car, keeping it waxed up and driving it for fun. During that time, I drove a sales vehicle for the company I was working with. So the car only had 17,000 miles on it when I sold it in 2003.

My income was down from the previous several years and so, although it was paid off, my wife asked me to sell it and I did. I was thinking about how I had sold it and tried to do so many other things to make our marriage better but none of it was working. Then I heard Pastor Hayford say a prayer, which really touched my soul. He suggested we pray for our families using this prayer:

> "I begin to cover my family, I begin to lay hold of what was done at the cross, that its power break whatever evil or human failure would seek to destroy our family, and the Glory of the Lord, that was the same Glory that attended their pathway out of Egypt, will begin to make a way of exodus for us! (Our Family)"

After listening to this sermon, I found myself saying, "Lord, I have tried to do everything that I know of to right this marriage, and nothing has worked. And I know Your way is the perfect way, that Your Will is perfect, and so I surrender my will to Your Will Lord. Whatever You show me to do I will do from this day forward."

As I said this, tears streamed down my face. They were tears of joy. I was overwhelmed by the Almighty presence of my Savior saving me. I knew something great had happened and I wanted to share it with somebody. So, I called my Mom and told her that I had surrendered my life to Jesus while listening to the cassette tape she had given me. I called my brother and shared with him the joy I felt and what I had done.

You have probably heard many testimonies of how and when people turned their life over to Jesus, but this is probably the first one you have heard of where it occurred while driving down the interstate! That shows there is not just one way to come to Christ. He will take you anytime and anyway, but you have to really want Him to come into your life. It has to come from your heart, mind, and soul.

While I had tried to accept Jesus while watching a TV evangelist earlier, it happened for me while driving down the road. And the best part was, that although it did not immediately save my marriage, my family could see a difference in me.

I started becoming a better husband and a better father. Slowly God began removing the pride that stood in the way of a better marriage, and He began changing me from the inside out. For me, and perhaps for many marriages, the best thing that can be done when you are going through a rough time in your marriage is to turn to Jesus, to submit to our Savior, and let His perfect will be lived out in our life as we daily surrender to Him. As the saying goes: "Let Go and Let God."

26. Date Your Wife

I recently attended a wedding where the priest delivered a nonconventional message. He stepped down from the altar area of the sanctuary into the pew area of the sanctuary and began talking to the congregation, imploring us to make time for what is important.

He was conveying this message to the bride and groom — but instead of looking at them, he had his back to them and was speaking to the congregation. My take on this was he was not just getting them to buy into this idea of dating your wife, but he was also trying to convince those in the church of the need to strengthen their marriages. Undoubtedly there were many in the congregation who did not regularly schedule a date night with their wives or husbands.

My pastor, Kevin Myers, has raised this discussion in his sermons from time-to-time at 12Stone Church. He says that he and his wife have a date night every week and believes it is critical to having a healthy marriage.

We normally hear this type of message at a wedding, but this is something that needs to be practiced often. Perhaps the bride and groom will never forget this message but we need to cling to its truth, too.

After the wedding, most people returned back to our busy schedules, and just as Christians keep just as busy schedules as non-Christians, we have about the same rate of divorce.

This priest went on to further analyze our society and explain that, in our society, communication is becoming more-and-more with our smartphones, tablets or computers. We are spending more time by ourselves and less in community, less with our family, and less with our spouse.

This priest challenged us by reminding us that just like playing tennis or any other activity, if we are to get good at it, we need to practice. We need to place a priority on marriage again and practice making it better by including a regular date night with our spouse.

I admit that there are some weeks that my wife and I don't have a "date night." But what I have found is this: the more time we spend together the better we get along.

When we can connect with the root of what really brought us together as a couple before we were married, and reestablish those ties through weekly date nights our marriage tends to prosper. So I encourage you, as I have learned from my pastor over the years and this priest recently at a wedding, to put a priority on dating your wife.

27. Men, Don't Be a Wimp

In biblical times, men were in leadership positions in most everything—churches, families, cities, and countries. Whereas, today women may hold leadership positions in all of these entities.

Women's involvement in church, government and other groups is a positive factor, yet it sometimes seems that as women have stepped up in the family to take a greater spiritual role more men have knowingly or unknowingly taken a step back as the spiritual leaders of the family.

In many families the husband does not come to church and so leaves the responsibility for bringing the children to church to the wife. Or it may be that the husband also attends church with the wife, but he leaves other religious duties to the mom—such as attendance at midweek services or getting younger children to youth church.

In many households, the woman is the one who sets the example in the family regarding prayer and devotion. But I don't read in the Bible where it tells husbands to delegate that responsibility to the wife. Rather in Scripture, I read that the responsibilities of the father include nurturing the spiritual growth of their children.

Consider "Fathers, do not exasperate your children; instead bring them up in the training and the instruction of the Lord." (Ephesians 6:4) The father, as head of the household does well to set the expectations for the family members—in regards to behavior, spirituality, and discipline.

A father could look beyond this Scripture for fathers to the Scripture for deacons as listed in 1 Timothy 3:4 where it says, "He must manage his own family well and see that his children obey him with proper respect."

Obviously, this would require an active role on the part of the father, including his involvement in disciplining their children—from their early years until they leave home. It also removes part of the burden from the wife, who typically has the parenting responsibilities if the husband takes the characteristic approach to raising his children.

28. Men, Save Your Marriage

Men, do you realize that it is your responsibility to keep your marriage healthy and to look after the health of your wife. This is commanded to us in Ephesians 5:23: "For the husband is the head of the wife as Christ is the head of the church, his body, of which he is the Savior."

This passage is primarily addressing the wife submitting to the husband as head of the family. But in The Life Application Bible footnote to this verse, the note addresses the fact that as head of the household the husband is to serve his wife just as Jesus served the disciples. The footnote reads, "According to the Bible, the man is the spiritual head of the family, and his wife should acknowledge his leadership." But real spiritual leadership involves service. Just as Christ served the disciples, even to the point of washing their feet, so the husband is to serve his wife.

Because we are to be the head of the wife, we should be concerned with every part of their health; physical, mental, and spiritual health, as if they are part of our own body. We are joined to our spouses. Genesis 2:24 says, "For this reason a man will leave his father and mother and be united to his wife, and they become one flesh."

If our wife is dealing with something emotional, we as the husband should sense this and try to assist her. Sometimes this will only be as a sounding board for her to release how she is feeling, with no input from the husband. I know this is difficult for men as men in general are problem solvers. Whereas women want to know they can express their feelings without being judged or told what they need to do.

I did not understand this for many years in my marriage until my wife told me that she just wanted someone she could verbalize her feelings to—it helped her process the particular issue. Sometimes she would even say, "I just want to express something to you, but I don't want a response." And so, as her husband who is one in body with her, I would listen and say nothing. Perhaps, if I felt so led, the next day or the next week I would gently suggest a possible solution. But I would honor her request and allow her to just express what she was feeling or the way she saw a certain situation.

Of course, there are additional verses in Ephesians 5 that confirm that husbands are to love their wives and support them in all circumstances. The apostle Paul reminds us, "Husbands, love your wives, just as Christ loved the church and gave himself up for her" (v. 25). He goes on to instruct the church, "In this same way, husbands ought to love their wives as their own bodies. He who loves his wife loves himself. After all, no one ever hated his own body, but he feeds and cares for it, just as Christ does the church."

The Life Application Bible footnote for verses 25-30 states, "Paul devotes twice as many words to telling husbands to love their wives as to telling wives to submit to their husbands. How should a man love his wife? (1) He should be willing to sacrifice everything for her. (2) He should make her well-being of primary importance. (3) He should care for her as he cares for his own body."

The theme that is abundantly clear in all of Ephesians 5 is that the husband is the head of the wife and must do everything within his power to support his wife and create a healthy lifestyle for her. Beyond the words here, the added emphasis I want to place upon the relationship between the husband and the wife is that it is the husband's responsibility to pursue the wife and never give up on his wife.

Think about it, God created men as the pursuers, whether pursuing food for the family through hunting or pursuing a woman through dating and courting. Think about the typical Walt Disney classics like Beauty and the Beast or Cinderella. It is the man who pursues the lady. If this is inherent to our nature as men, we should continue this approach not just during courtship but after the marriage also.

Living out Ephesians 5 there should never be disunity between the husband and wife. But we live in a fallen world, and in almost all marriages there is division at times. When those times arise, it should be the husband who is the pursuer in keeping the marriage together. The husband should do as it says in the Life Application Bible footnote for Ephesians 5:25-30,

"He should be willing to sacrifice everything for her." If we as husbands pursue this in our marriages I think we will find, as I have found, that doing so endears our wives to us.

Suggested Prayer:

Father in Heaven, you know all things. You created us as man, and then out of man's ribs, You created woman. You put into us our desire for a mate. You tell us in your Word that when we marry You join us together as one. In the name of Jesus, help us to live out what that means in marriage each day. Help us to die to self and put our spouse first. Help us to always want the best for our spouse. We ask Father that You will fill us with Your Spirit and remove our selfish desires, so that we might act outside of our nature and love others more than ourselves. Father, we ask especially that You will place in each husband's heart unbounded love and concern for his spouse. We ask Father, that You will help husbands to care for their wives just as they care for their own bodies. Finally, we ask that when division arises in the marriage relationship that husbands will never give up, but rather pursue their bride as Christ did the Church. In the name of Jesus we pray all these things, knowing that if we believe, You will give us the desires of our heart. Amen.

Gold Nuggets
to Open Up
the Heavens

29. Praying for the Future

We all pray, but do we realize that prayer reveals so much about our walk with Jesus. I believe most Christians do not pray often for things that might occur three, five or twenty years in the future. But God wants us to pray continuously, and if we have developed our prayer life to pray for long periods of time, we will probably be praying for more than just the current events of our lives.

Our minds will think ahead and we will pray about our future. For those approaching retirement (like myself), that will most likely enter our prayers as we get closer and closer to this stage of life.

About eight years ago I felt that I should ask for the Lord's guidance and protection before going on trips. I solicited the help of my prayer partner, my brother Ron, and he joined me in prayer for these periods of travel.

We often prayed months in advance of the trips. I have continued this practice and have felt God's blessings on my family's travels. One trip in particular was made to Florida about eight years ago, when we stayed in a beachfront condominium.

The trip was made in late May or early June and it just seemed like everything went better than we even hoped for. My wife and I along with our three daughters were able to observe sea turtles, crawling up on the shoreline at this beachfront condominium the evening we arrived.

We had never seen this before and we learned that this only happens for several months each year. It was dark when we arrived from Atlanta and after unpacking we went down to take a walk on the beach. This sea turtle emerged out of the water to lay its eggs about five minutes after we went down to the beach.

To experience nature in this fashion was truly special and it definitely got our trip off to a great start—and it continued throughout the week. While walking down the beach a day or two later we saw two manatees swimming very close to shore. They were in water that was only three or four feet deep, so we walked out to them and they engaged in almost childlike play with us.

They swam around us and even brushed up against us. They were slowly swimming down the beachfront parallel to the shoreline towards an intercostal water inlet. And so we walked in the water for about 500 yards or so as they swam along beside us, occasionally looping around us in a circle and brushing up to us.

The best part of this is that we experienced something that even most of the permanent residents of the condominium had never experienced. We spoke to several residents who informed us that they had never seen the manatees in the ocean before, only in the warmer, intercostal waterways.

God had gifted us with an experience on this trip that few, if any, residents had experienced. I believe the only reason we were able to experience this fantastic vacation week was because of the power of prayers that started many weeks and months in advance.

Since this habit of praying in advance yielded great results for many trips for our family, I began praying in advance for other things. One example was that I prayed in advance for the decision my daughters would make as to which college to attend. I suggest you just pray for what is on your heart, and trust that our God is big enough to handle all of your prayers—those for today, and those you make today for your future tomorrow.

30. The Power of Focused Prayer

There is power in focused, specific prayer. I have heard this from many sound and committed Christians, and so as I began to write on this topic, I dwelt on this practice for a few moments. I felt God directing my thoughts and words regarding this gold nugget.

So, if God knows everything, why is our focused, specific prayer more powerful and effective than an overall, general prayer? In my dwelling on this idea, God brought to mind the fact that He is our Heavenly Father. As our Heavenly Father, we should approach Him as we would our earthly father or mother. When we desire something and approach our earthly parent, we do not typically beat around the bush. The normal approach of a child is go and ask the parent for what they want. When a daughter goes shopping and finds a dress she really likes, she shows it to the parent and says, "This is the one I want."

In this scenario, there's rarely any doubt about what the child wants. I believe the situation with the dress is similar to the situation of asking our Heavenly Father for something. We can pray in generalities without having to spend much thought about the prayer, without investing much effort or forethought about what we are praying for.

I believe God wants us to be fully convicted about what we bring to Him in prayer. I also believe He wants us to have given it much forethought, that it shouldn't be a generic lukewarm prayer, but it should be something that is important to us—something that we have thought deeply on and we are eager to plead our case to Him. It must be important to us if we are coming to Him in prayer about it. So we should know exactly what we want, just like the girl who chose the dress she wanted.

The power of focused prayer draws from the same principle as in our repentance or confession for sins. It is not enough to simply approach God with a confession, simply stating, "God, please forgive me for anything that I may have done wrong today." Rather, when we ask God to forgive us we should identify specifically what we did wrong, and then ask God to forgive us of that particular sin.

The principle is to identify exactly what we are asking for and then take that exact issue to God for His blessing or for His forgiveness. Being specific makes our request or confession more powerful.

Rather than praying a general "catch-all" prayer like, "God, please give me good health." We should open our hearts up to Him and pray with expectancy and with focus. "Catch-all" prayers don't require much time or effort. But when there is cancer attacking one of the organs in our body, we innately become specific in praying for the cancer growth to be stopped in that organ and for the cancer to go into remission.

I am grateful for a time in the last couple of years where focused, specific prayer was answered in my life. I had my retina detach in my left eye three times over a period of about 4 months. My vision at times was only 20/200 after surgery. I was praying for my eye to heal, but I wasn't praying with conviction, telling God exactly what I wanted, so my vision had stabilized in the left eye at about 20/70.

Because I am a home inspector, good eyesight was much needed so I resolved to tell God exactly what I wanted. I thanked God for restoring my eyesight to 20/70, knowing that many who have detached retina surgeries only have 20/150 or 20/200 vision afterwards. But I told the Lord that I knew He could do anything. I knew He wanted to bless me, and I believed I could have 20/20 vision.

I continued to pray that prayer in faith, and I did everything that I could for the eye to heal, like beginning to take fish oil daily (which has Omega 3 in it). I am thankful to tell you that after a couple months of praying like this, God did indeed answer my prayer. My vision in my right eye is about 20/30 and in my left eye, the one which had three detached retinas, improved to be greater than that in my right eye, to 20/20.

I believe this concept of praying focused prayers in the appropriate circumstances is precisely what God would have us to do. When we are having a relationship issue with one person, it is appropriate to pray deliberately for that one relationship.

We certainly could pray for God to bless all of our relationships, but if we pray focused prayers on one issue, delving deeply and explaining soundly what we want and what we would like God to do, I believe it not only will be pleasing to God, it will be pleasing to us. Another example would be about praying after a natural disaster (like a hurricane or tornado).

If we pray for specific actions rather than a general prayer to just "Help the people," I believe it will lend more credence to our prayers. It all hinges on the time and effort we put into our prayers. We are told in the Bible "to pray without ceasing." So the more effort and time we put into our prayers, the closer we are to following the example of Christ.

We know that while in the Garden of Gethsemane—prior to Jesus' arrest—that He left John and Peter to pray. Jesus was praying specifically about the immediate task before Him, His arrest, torture, and crucifixion. We know from the Bible that part of His specific, focused prayer was, "Father, if you are willing, take this cup from me; yet not my will, but yours be done" (Luke 22:42). Verse 44 says, "Being in anguish, [Jesus] prayed more earnestly, and his sweat was like drops of blood falling to the ground."

Here we see the demonstration of our Savior, Jesus Christ, praying specifically for what lay immediately ahead. We can model our prayers after the example here in Luke of how Jesus faced His impending crisis with fervent, focused prayer.

31. Are You Seeing the Work of the Holy Spirit in Your Life?

Are you looking for and recognizing the work of the Holy Spirit in your life? Do you praise God for the good ways in which he works in your life. I am constantly amazed at God's goodness, on the blessings he pours out on us even while we are still sinners and have fallen short of His perfect will for us.

I believe the Holy Spirit is at work in each person's life but that only a few recognize He is at work in their life and the signs of the Holy Spirit for them. If we are busy we may miss the work and signs of the Holy Spirit in our lives. Creating margins or blank areas in our schedules provides the openings for the Holy Spirit to be revealed to us and for us to recognize His presence.

The signs of the Holy Spirit can be totally different in one person's life versus another's. In 2007, my brother Ron was very generous and extended an offer of an expense paid trip to Israel for my family and I along with about seven other immediate family members.

As I prayed in preparation for that trip, I asked God to show me one sign that I would know the Holy Spirit was with us. God answered that prayer when we were on the Mount of Olives.

There was a church locked up behind a brick wall there that we visited and while taking a picture of my wife and daughters with my Mom I looked up and there was a white dove on the gutter of the church that was looking down at us. As the Holy Spirit is represented by a dove, I knew in my soul immediately that the dove, was the answer to my prayer. I felt a feeling of joy come over me as I dwelled on the moment in which the Holy Spirit had shown me He was with me and answered my prayer.

Many years thereafter, I began noticing cardinals in my yard. I particularly liked and was drawn to watch these birds. I also noticed that more than other species of birds they generally travel in pairs. By this I mean that when I saw one in my yard, I generally saw the opposite sex cardinal nearby.

I thought to myself, Wow isn't it cool that out of all the birds I typically see the cardinal is probably the most beautiful, and God made them so they like to stay close together as a couple. That is how I desire my relationship with my wife to be, that we do as many things as we can together.

Then I started noticing when I received a revelation from God or had a high point in my daily devotion that often it would be immediately followed by a cardinal or cardinals coming into view. I realized, that for me, the presence of cardinals typically signifies the Holy Spirit is with me.

In April of 2017, I went to a prophetic conference, which my wife did not go to and we discussed before my leaving that we should try to spend time together on Sunday afternoon when I returned. When I returned we decided to go on a walk in the neighborhood and there were literally about eight cardinals flying about us as we began our walk. I remarked to Lisa that symbolizes the presence of the Holy Spirit. I guess the Holy Spirit's presence, which was strong during the prophetic conference, was still with me even after I returned home.

Have you noticed anything of nature that surrounds you signifying the presence of the Holy Spirit? I have heard for some people a butterfly signifies to them the presence of the Holy Spirit.

Recently I have learned that other types of birds can represent the Holy Spirit and that birds in general represent messengers, blessings or gifts. I have also learned that the color of the bird is significant.

While at the prophetic conference, during prayer time, the minister of prayer commented that there was a bluebird on a railing just outside the prayer room. For those who are unfamiliar with the appearance of a bluebird it has vivid blue wings and a head of blue with orange on the belly. They are beautiful birds and the minister commented that the bluebird seemed to show up when there were special times during prayer.

There are obviously other signs and wonders which God uses to let us know that He or the Holy Spirit is at work around us. Some of these are subtle, others are profound, such as when I saw the white dove at the church in Israel.

I encourage you as you grow in your walk with God to look for confirmation that the Holy Spirit is with you. It may be as simple as the harmony or unity of a gathering of people where you sense the presence of His Presence creating a unique environment of togetherness, cooperation, joy, or peace. When you sense it quickly praise God in your mind for the workings of the Holy Spirit, for it is good to praise Him for the blessings we receive.

I am particularly amazed at the way God brought this book into being. I am not only amazed by the way he spoke to me to have me begin this journey, but also by His faithfulness to see the book through to completion. It was amazing to see the way he orchestrated all the contacts needed to make this book come into being. He knew all of the connections all of the people that needed to be knit together to lead me, who had never written a book, to the path of the publisher.

The Holy Spirit's leading me through this process began with my joining a home inspection group dedicated to mentoring those in the industry. This company was called the millionaire inspector community and was started by a home inspector who wanted home inspectors to learn from each other and grow their business to the point that it might be generating revenue of a million dollars per year.

I decided to join not because I expected my business to make a million a year, but because through the community of inspectors and the discussions between them I knew I could reap greater efficiency in my business through being a part of this community.

As a natural process of becoming involved in this group, I went to a convention they organized where a publicist spoke. About six months later the Holy Spirit laid it on my heart to write this book. I contacted this publicist who put me in touch with an associate who could do a one page promotional flyer on my proposed book. Only a portion of this book was complete but this one-page was distributed and generated interest at the Book Exposition America in New York City.

I continued writing on this book but stopped during the summer when I was very busy inspecting houses. I forgot to pick back up on my writing until in January when my pastor led a sermon about "re-enlisting." What he meant by "re-enlisting" was to pick back up on something that God had placed on your heart at one time, and I knew this message had particular significance for me.

Then it was time for editing and I needed contacts for an editor and so through my church I explored a couple of opportunities but those did not yield an editor. But, a former client kept getting in touch with me about questions concerning the house he had purchased. One day while I was at his home, I expressed the need for an editor. He's a pastor and a very wise man. He told me that his father had written 19 books and used several editors.

Some of the editors he referred me to were busy on other projects and could not become involved with mine, but they kept referring me to other people they knew who were editors. Eventually, I found the one that I needed and if you look at the connection of people it is probably over 10 or 11 people in the chain before I got to the final one! God had a plan just as He has one for you, too.

32. Are You "Extra"?

My wife Lisa and I drove my daughter and three other college students back to college the weekend after spring break was over in March 2017. The students were doing the majority of the talking while occasionally my wife or I would interject or ask a question or add something to the discussion.

We drove about four hours and as the students were talking the discussion would bounce from one of their friends to another friend. They were discussing some of their friends and one of them made a comment that this friend was "extra."

My wife Lisa's curiosity piqued and she asked "what is an 'extra'"? They thought for a moment and then said an "extra" is someone that is over the top. Someone that takes things too far or farther than the normal person. After talking about this for some time they concurred that performing arts individuals like those involved with drama or dance have a greater inclination to be "extra."

My question for you is are you an "extra" for God? Do you take things of God further than the typical Christian? Do you put God first before all other things or is God just something you just take out on Sunday and worship him for an hour or so.

I think the definition of an "extra" for God would be someone who lets God permeate their soul so that they are living, breathing, and moving in the Holy Spirit. Someone that when others see this person they say this person is overflowing with God and you cannot help but notice.

These type of people will impact nonbelievers as the nonbelievers will see and hear and sense something different about these "extras" for God. That is what God calls us to do — to go out into the world and make disciples of all nations. We are to be salt and light to a society that is far from Christ so that when they encounter us they realize we are different.

But we must not be critical, we must not be condemning, but rather we must be warm and welcoming so that others are attracted to us not repelled by our convictions. We still must stand firm on our convictions but we must do it like Jesus did walking through the countryside where people were attracted to him.

Where he would tell them things they wanted to hear — good things not bad things. He was not critical of the woman accused of adultery. Even when the Pharisees brought her to Jesus and told Him she was caught in the very act of adultery, Jesus offered her new life and eternal hope.

So we must not be critical to others but must be loving — overflowing with the love of Jesus so that others are attracted to us just as they were with Jesus. Therefore, if there is one thing that you should be "extra" about, it's extra passionate for everything related to Jesus. Others should be able to know that we are extra for Jesus for with that extra comes extra blessings as we grow closer and closer to Jesus.

Suggested Prayer:

Lord help us to be "extras" for you. Help us to be sold out to Jesus. Help us to know what to do in every situation and fill us with your words so that we can go into this society that is far from you and be salt and light. Help us to be a strong voice and a welcoming voice not a voice of terror or condemnation, but instead of love and peace and joy and all of the fruit of the spirit. Help us to be abounding in steadfast love not just for those who are like us and know you, but for the lost, the broken-hearted, those addicted to drugs or alcohol. For in showing love to ones such as these we may bring heaven to earth and bring many here on earth into your kingdom, in Jesus name we pray.

33. Tear Down the Walls

God has been impressing upon me in the first half of 2017 that Satan has a hold on many people, and there is a wall separating them from the love of God. The love of God is still there, and is always available to those who seek Him to draw them closer to Himself. But many have been blinded by Satan and are living far from God. They have a wall of sin separating themselves from God.

The love of God is still flowing out from the Father but much of it is blocked by the sin in their life, which is represented by the wall. Still God is in the business of tearing down the walls, of seeking the least and the lost, and in restoration. He desires that all should be saved and He desires that we who are saved have an active role in bringing this about. We are commanded by Jesus to go and make disciples throughout all of the world. When we see those who are trapped in sin, it is our calling to share the hope we have that will free them from all that entraps them.

We need to acknowledge that all have sinned but also recognize that many are living in bondage to sin. Living in bondage to sin distances a person from the love of God and the blessings that he seeks to bestow on them.

Perhaps some of those we recognize as living in bondage to sin are our family members and we know they are far from God. This may be causing these family members hardships, which in turn causes our hearts to yearn for them to be connected to God. We desire that they should live within God's decrees and commandments.

Or perhaps they are our neighbors or friends who are living apart from God. How do we tear down these walls that separate them from the love of God and perhaps their eternal destiny?

There are many ways to help those who are lost, but perhaps the best way would be through intercessory prayer. We can accomplish a lot by being the hands and feet of God and personally helping those we encounter and reaching out to those around us.

But what if in addition to these Godly steps we put into play intercessory prayer? After all we can only be in one place at one time, and the needs are so great, and the number of people that are far from God is so numerous. Which leads me to believe the most productive use of our time is to take up intercessory prayer, where we come before God and lift up in intercessory prayer for individuals and entire groups.

For example we can pray for a student we know is using drugs and all students at the high school or college using drugs or even all of them in a community. Or we could pray for one we know who is involved in pornography at a local high school and for God to work to bring down all the pornography addictions at the high school.

Because Jesus died on the cross and shed His blood for us, those of us who are born again have power through His sacrifice, power that comes through the Holy Spirit. With this power we can intercede and overcome all the power or the enemy. In the book of Revelations, we are reminded that we are kings and priests and we reign on earth! "You have made them to be a kingdom and priests to serve our God, and they will reign on earth." (Revelation 5:10)

The problem for much of this world is that Satan has deceived them into believing he has more power than we have as followers of Christ. We succumb to his ploys and tactics instead of trusting in the power we have through Jesus to overcome.

So if we live out what it says in Revelations, we should intercede for those that are deceived, for that is what priests do, they intercede. We can intercede and claim the power over Satan for he is a fallen angel.

We on the other hand are joint heirs with Christ, and have power over all of the enemy through Christ. We can decree or proclaim that Satan and any demonic forces be loosed from an individual or area for what we loose on earth is loosed in Heaven.

Satan is a defeated foe, but he has made many inroads into the lives of individuals, who have ceded authority to him through his accusations, deceit, and temptations. As believers, we have the power to step in, intercede, and overcome all the power of the enemy.

What an awesome feeling that is to know that God wants us to rule and reign on this earth, not Satan, and that he has given us the authority to do exactly that. To fulfill God's desires we need to live that out and intercede for those we know and see along with entire groups and areas, and decree their deliverance in Jesus' name.

34. Pray For Your Child(ren) Prior to Birth

I remember how excited I was when my wife Lisa and I made the decision to try and have a baby. We had been married for two years and were thoroughly enjoying being a married couple. Lisa had always enjoyed children and came from a family of three siblings, while I came from a family with four. After deciding we were ready for children, we both anxiously awaited the day our first child would be born.

I remember us praying for the health of the baby and of Lisa. This was not a one-time prayer but was an ongoing prayer during Lisa's pregnancy. I don't think we had the foresight at that point to pray for our children's future. We didn't pray for their high school or college years, or for their future spouses.

But later, after all three of our children were born, I heard a friend of mine telling a story of how his father-in-law prayed for his daughter's future husband before his daughter was even born. That really impressed me; this man had such foresight and fortitude to pray for his future son-in-law on behalf of his unborn daughter, and to pray for blessing for his daughter and future spouse.

I was impacted so deeply by this story that I had to decide what I would do going forward. I wished that I had said that prayer before my daughters were born, but I certainly could pray for my daughters' future spouses going forward. While we definitely have plenty to pray for in our current lives I encourage you look beyond your current situations - to pray into the future for blessings for you and your family. As I have put this into practice I have derived tremendous joy in the practice. I pray that you also will experience great joy in your future for your prayers in the present.

35. Pray For Family Unity

Our three daughters are almost exactly three years apart in age. We are very blessed that they love and care for one another the way they do. They enjoy spending quality time doing things with each other.

Although they each have their own full-sized bed, when all three are together, two of the three generally sleep together. Many times all three will squeeze into one of their full-sized beds because they like being with each other.

Lisa and I are blessed to have this harmony between our daughters. I know in many families there is discord between siblings. For this reason I believe it is important to pray for there to be harmony between your future children before they are even born.

Just as an earlier gold nugget suggested praying for your unborn children and particularly for their future spouses, I think we as parents should pray for family unity both before our children are born and daily after they are born. We should pray a shield of protection be placed over our children to shield them from the worldly ways, and pray for God's blessing to be on each of them and between them.

What a blessing it will be in our later stages of life to have our children come and visit us, and have a time of the celebration and enjoyment rather than discord and dysfunction. Yes, prayers for family unity, both before and after our children are born, will yield the type of blessings on the entire family that we can all enjoy.

36. Fasting

Several gold nuggets in this book pertain to praying and this gold nugget, fasting, is a complimentary nugget to those on praying. Fasting is mentioned in the Bible many times, typically when something important was desired. It was employed by those in the Old Testament and the New Testament alike. And while it was utilized quite frequently in the Bible, it seems we have gotten away from fasting to the point that it is a rare occurrence in today's society, even among evangelical Christians.

To discuss the practice of fasting, I referred to the dictionary for an accurate definition. The verb tense of the word "fast" is defined in the Merriam-Webster dictionary as "to abstain from food or to eat sparingly or abstain from some foods."

In a spiritual sense, the "fast" does not have to be from food. For example, during Lent many people "fast" from watching television or from surfing the internet. Primarily when speaking of fasting we are speaking of fasting from food. Many "fast" from sweets during the 40 days of Lent. But what I am encouraging in this gold nugget is fasting for a purpose, to supplement prayers for a cause with fasting.

I believe our prayer life would be elevated dramatically if we would incorporate fasting into our prayer practices, particularly when the larger, more significant issues or crises come up in our lives. Remember when the disciples came to Jesus and told them that they could not heal a man?

Jesus told them with some spirits they cannot be sent out strictly by praying, but that by prayer and fasting He was able to accomplish the casting out of the spirit and the healing of the person. So also with our trials and tribulations, not every obstacle requires fasting, but when the larger, more significant ones come along we would do well to "fast and pray."

There have been times in the past when I would "fast" more than once a week, and I felt the hand of God empowering me as a result of my prayers and fasting. But I want to admit that I have been remiss in my practice of fasting for the last couple of years—until the last year when I believe God has revealed to me the need to fast, particularly for our country. So I have been getting back into the habit of fasting. God has been gracious to me these times when I have fasted by filling me with His Spirit to guide me and answer my prayers.

Many people are unfamiliar with the practice of fasting, and they do not know how to begin or what to do during a "fast." There are many ways to "fast" and so I will discuss a few options. See if any of these resonate with you that you might employ for specific occasions to supplement your prayers.

First, you will probably want to discuss the idea of fasting with your doctor to determine if there are any health concerns that need to be considered. For myself, I have had borderline hypoglycemia, so complete fasting from all foods for any length of time is difficult, but I have done this on occasion when I do not have to be working or driving a vehicle. But what I typically do is "fast" from all foods for shorter periods of time—like for morning and lunch.

I do "fast" for longer periods of time, three days or longer, if I am employing only a "partial fast," where I will eat many foods but abstain from some. This can involve going on a "fast" where you do not eat any meat, or any sweets, or where the only thing you eat is clear liquids such as soup broth, white apple juice, etc.

One "fast" I have employed that seems to work well for me is where I abstain from all foods other than bread. During this "fast" I carry a package of bread with me in my car as I drive around, and I eat a slice or two at various times during the day when I feel my blood sugar dropping. A caution—continue to drink fluids during any "fast" so you do not become dehydrated.

Finally, it is suggested by many that after coming off of a "fast" that you slowly re-introduce food back into your system, rather than celebrating your "fast" by eating a large amount of food because you are hungry! As you "fast" more frequently, you will learn what works with your body the best while you see God at work in the issues you are fasting for.

In looking up the definition for "fast" in the dictionary, I found it of particular significance that the definition for the adverb "fast" was "so as to be hard to move, firmly or securely or immovable or fixedly." This struck me as a great illustration to the fact that when we "fast," God allows us to hold fast to whatever we are praying for. God can empower us and make us immovable or fixed in our faith for what we believe in and are praying for.

37. The Mature and Complete Christian

As Christians, it should be natural to desire to have a closer relationship with God and to feel His presence in our lives. We want to feel sure that when we pray He will answer our prayers. And yet we know the day someone turns his or her life over to Christ, they are not immediately a mature Christian.

I think we could all agree that the growth of a Christian is a process in which God grows us up and shares more and more of His wisdom with us over the years of time.

When researching this gold nugget I found it interesting that the heading on www.BibleGateway.com was "trials and temptations." In speaking with other Christians who I consider mature and complete, I found that many times when they have gone through trials in their lives their faith is strengthened. So while we would all like to be mature and complete Christians without going through the tough stuff, this is rarely the way God works in the life of a believer. Consider the words from James 1:2-8.

> Consider it pure joy, my brothers, whenever you face trials of many kinds, because you know that the testing of your faith produces perseverance. Perseverance must finish its work so that you may be mature and complete, not lacking anything. If any of you lacks wisdom, he should ask God, who gives generously to all without finding fault, and it will be given to him. But when he asks, he must believe and not doubt, because he who doubts is like a wave of the sea, blown and tossed by the wind. That man should not think he will receive anything from the Lord; he is a double minded man, unstable in all he does.

The way I read this is that developing faith is like learning to play tennis. No one playing tennis the first time expects to get the tennis ball in the service box every time. It takes practice, and more practice to consistently serve the ball into the service box area.

Likewise, the first time we pray we don't know how everything is going to work and so we do not expect to receive an immediate answer to that prayer. But with time when we see our prayers being answered, we will believe and not doubt. Then we can expect to receive what we asked of the Lord. So we should consider it pure joy when we face trials because those trials test our faith and produce perseverance.

As we successfully move beyond our trials and tribulations, we become mature and complete Christians. As mature and complete Christians, we can ask God for wisdom and understanding. We learn to trust Him without doubt and we know He will provide us with the wisdom we seek. And just like the tennis professional who is mature and ready to compete on the highest level, we must continue to practice daily the activities and practices that strengthen our faith.

38. Do Your Part

This gold nugget refers to the fact that while in faith we can look to God to answer our prayers, there are responsibilities we have in praying. For example, we must pray in line with God's will. In other words, what we are praying for needs to bring glory to God.

In my life, at one point I had three surgeries on my left eye for three detached retinas, and so I prayed for better eyesight. After surgery it was 20/200 and then it stabilized to 20/70. I believed God would make my vision better and prayed for Him to do this, but was told by my eye doctors that taking fish oil would help get the proper nutrients (Omega 3) to the eye to help in the healing.

The doctor had a partnership with a company that provided high quality liquid fish oil to their clients, so I placed an order and began taking this fish oil. Over time my vision improved to 20/20 in the eye and so while believing that God did a miracle in healing my eye, I have also continued to take the fish oil daily, while it was healing.

Healing my eye brought glory to God as I professed to others that I believed that God would restore my vision, but I was also willing to do everything within my capabilities—including taking the fish oil daily. Another way of thinking of this is to think about an individual who is attempting to quit drinking and praying to God about it.

If on their way home from work each day they stop at a bar and have several drinks, it is not appropriate for them to say, "I prayed to God to make me quit drinking and nothing happened."

They could try driving a different way home if it is too tempting to drive their normal way that passes by their favorite bar. But they have a responsibility in their prayer also. Or say someone is trying to lose weight but they frequently go out to eat at an "all you can eat" restaurant. It wouldn't be right for them to complain they couldn't lose weight or that God wasn't answering their prayers. So do what God would have you do and expect God to do the rest.

39. Heal Yourself? Yes!

A re we believing too much in the power of medicine? With all the marvels of medicine and high tech medical equipment, I am afraid we are relying on everything but Jesus to heal us when we are sick or in pain. Many times, when we have a pain in our body the first thing we do is to reach for pain pills or make an appointment with a chiropractor or physical therapist.

We exclude God from the options of how to eliminate or ease our pain. But if you pause for a minute and think about it, you might find yourself wondering if this really is the way God intended it? Are we relying on God to be our healer? Or have we veered away from that mindset to a new system that relies on ways of man and not the ways of God? I know that He uses doctors in powerful way. Luke in the Bible was a physician. But I also wonder if we have let our secular society set norms, which we now follow.

I believe that God wants each of us to put our confidence and trust in Him and believe that He is the great physician who brings healing and hope. The Bible tells us of the power we have because Christ died for us and how that power is available for many things—including healing.

Consider the words found in Luke 10:19: "I have given you authority to trample on snakes and scorpions and to overcome all the power of the enemy; nothing will harm you." If this is true (which we know all Scripture is true), are we exercising that authority which Jesus already gave us? Do we trust in these words and believe we have the power to heal ourselves?

Remember the story of the woman who trusted and believed that Jesus could heal her? She just touched the hem of Jesus' garment and she was healed. As told in Mark 5:34, "He said to her, 'Daughter, your faith has healed you. Go in peace and be freed from your suffering.'"

Another example of faith leading to healing is the story of the centurion whose servant was paralyzed. He came to Jesus seeking healing for his servant. This story is found in the 8th chapter of Matthew, and I include verses 6-8 and 13 for illustration.

> "'Lord,' [the centurion] said, 'my servant lies at home paralyzed and in terrible suffering.' Jesus said to him, 'I will go and heal him.' The centurion replied, 'Lord, I do not deserve to have you come under my roof. But just say the word, and my servant will be healed.' Then Jesus said to the centurion, 'Go! It will be done just as you believed it would.' And his servant was healed at that very hour."

Here again, because of faith, his servant was healed. While in both of these stories Jesus was present, there are many other stories of the disciples healing individuals after Jesus' death, and the Scripture quoted above from Luke tells us that WE have the same power. We just need to exercise that authority.

I have exercised this authority and have been healed on two physical issues after many months (even years) of medical problems. Until I had this revelation, that if we believe, we have the power to heal ourselves I was burdened down with what I told people was a bad back. This began in 2003 and progressively got worst until I couldn't sit for more than 5 or 10 minutes without pain. Then, by the grace of God I listened to two CD sets on Spiritual Laws that govern the different types of prayer, by Randall Grier.

I learned that if you believe, and act like you believe, God is more than willing to answer our prayers. But previous to this, I would pray for my back, but then tell people I had a bad back. In essence, I was nullifying my own prayers by saying I have (and will continue to have) a bad back. When I repented and began believing God would heal my back, and I started telling people I believed that He was healing my back—He did. Now I can sit for hours without pain and I don't take Ibuprofen like I used to do.

More amazing is the miraculous healing of my left eye. This healing happened in the fall of 2014. I had surgery for a detached retina in this eye three times in 2014. My eyesight was as bad as 20/200 at some points after the surgeries. It improved slowly to 20/70 but I was told it would not get any better. The eye doctor told me that the very best my eyes would ever see would be 20/70.

I continued to believe God would restore my vision. I prayed and believed He would do so. When others asked how my vision was, I told them I believed my eyesight would continue to improve. God restored my vision to 20/20 in that eye, so I don't even need glasses. When I told my optometrist the story, he tells me it is a miracle because he was the one who referred me to a specialist who performed a special test that indicated the best my retina could read was 20/70.

I believe one reason we have such a prevalence of physical and mental woes is because we don't believe in and trust the words of God, related to healing. When most of us have a pain or illness, our first instinct is not to stop and pray, believing God will heal us of whatever ails us. But that should be our first response, to turn to God in prayer or to reach out to a prayer group asking for prayers. Although I experienced the miraculous healing in 2014, there were nuances regarding the prayer of faith and healing that played out over years.

I invite you to join me in believing and practicing prayers that get answered regarding our health and other issues. Who knows? There may be issues bothering you, which God is prepared to eliminate when you will turn to Him and believe that He has a better life for you—just as He did for me!

Gold Nuggets to Create Order & Discipline

40. Journaling

One of the most positive steps I have taken in the last five years to strengthening my faith and just plain feeling good and blessed has come as I have begun to journal regularly.

Oh, I had journaled on occasion in the past — while on a mission trip to Honduras and on a family vacation to Israel, which was enjoyable. But as I began journaling, I found myself writing less about what I was doing, and more about what God was doing in my life.

Our pastor originally mentioned journaling suggesting it to our congregation. He said that we could write what we are thankful for, what prayers are answered, and the way we see God at work in our lives. Little did I know how significant his suggestion would become in my personal devotional life.

Journaling can take many forms and I believe there is no one form that fits all individuals. I believe the best approach is a contingent approach depending on the individual. Some like recording the information on a computer, some on notebook paper.

I have found satisfaction in buying a Christian journal bound in a nice binding which allows me to appreciate the significance of the journal before I even begin writing inside. Some may only record spiritual thoughts and prayers, others may elect to record personal happenings also.

I like to include what I am thankful to God for and thoughts I have about how God is leading me as well as occasional references to personal events in mine and my family's lives. You may decide to include how you are feeling about something going on in your life, or what is happening in the world around us. Regardless of the approach or format, taking the time to journal, to slow down and reflect, may give you the added perspective that is needed as you strive for a deeper spiritual connection with God.

I want to share with you the joy I found as I read in my journal previous writings from a dark period in my life. My mother had passed away from cancer in 2012. My journal reflected those difficult days when I consciously chose to look for God in the midst of the darkness of that struggle.

> "Thank you God, for confirming to me… the right hospice company…"

> "Thank you for letting me register Mom into Hospice…For hearing her share with the hospice representative how she thinks us four boys (her four sons) have taken good care of her…Also, Lord thank you for allowing me to hear how food no longer tastes good to her. But I brought her favorite, strawberry shortcake, and she ate a slice of it. Thank you Lord, for arranging my home inspection schedule so that I could schedule two days this week with Mom…"

Reviewing my journal now, years after she has died, gives me great peace and comfort. Reading about those last days of her life, and my reaction to them, refreshes my memory and strengthens my faith that God was there, leading us through that difficult time.

I find this part of journaling — this reading of earlier entries from time to time — to be one of the most gratifying benefits of writing. It becomes a faith building exercise that often erupts into tears of joy as I grasp the depths of His faithfulness. Because I have experienced it I can draw on this knowledge that He is faithful as I journal daily.

By reading previous passages, I see the amazing hand of God at work in our family, weaving a thread of His faithfulness through our prayers, knitting them together in His wonderful providence. His answers to our request have been far better than we had ever imagined. Even recording difficult life experiences — such as the death of a loved one or a specific hardship — provides a basis for significant emotional processing.

Journaling can also be a tool through which God brings satisfaction and joy, peace and closure, or even relief from crushing grief. Mountaintop experiences are much sweeter when you look back and see that God was at work in the dark. I encourage you to journal regularly and often. Even if you cannot put pen to paper daily, writing a few sentences a few times a week will still yield ample opportunities to look back and see the movement of a gracious God who loves us and who is at work in our lives.

41. Keep the Sabbath Holy

The Pew Research Center and the Gallup Poll report data from 2013 indicating the percentage of Americans that attend church on a weekly basis is 37 and 39 percent, respectively.

In this gold nugget I want us to explore the fact that God commanded us in the Ten Commandments to observe the Sabbath and keep it holy, and according to this data, the majority of Americans do not even take an hour or two out of their Sunday to go to church.

Undoubtedly there are some who do observe the Sabbath, and utilize the whole day to rest and refrain from everyday activities. My estimate of the percentage of Americans that do would be 10 percent or less. This may be one of the reasons why God's favor appears to have been withdrawn from the United States. I can think of many of the other Ten Commandments that are not being kept by Americans, but this one certainly has significance.

There are varying opinions about how the Sabbath should be kept since the advent of Jesus. Many think that since Jesus "did away with the (Jewish) law", that we are allowed to work on the Sabbath.

Others believe we should not work on the Sabbath. But all seem to agree that the intention for Christians is that the Sabbath should be a day of rest, worship, and rejuvenation. We should honor God on that day by setting it apart from all other days of the week, and think of Him throughout the day. We should praise Him for everything that He does for us.

Many deeply religious people, including pastors, work on Sunday. But they generally plan to take one of the other six days of the week off so that they do observe a Sabbath every week.

I remember that at the time I received Jesus Christ as my personal Savior, I was listening to a Focus on the Family recording, and the founder, James Dobson, was sharing that he had been working seven days a week and had resolved that he needed to get back to working no more than six days a week.

I pray that you honor God on the Sabbath. I especially pray that you worship Him well during the one or two hours you are in church and that you resolve to make a commitment to weekly church attendance a regular portion of your Sabbath Day activities.

42. Stay On Task

This is one of my biggest challenges — staying on task. A big emphasis in today's world is placed on multitasking, but I think that just exacerbates this problem of staying on task.

I think it is the symptom of the business of this world we live in. I feel like I have so many responsibilities it is hard to get everything done completely. It is a struggle to complete each job before a higher priority sprouts up, which I am eager to jump to and address.

Fortunately for me when it comes to this book project, I sense that God gave me a second chance. You see, I was initially given the thought for the book during my devotion time on February 28, 2014. I even wrote down the title of the book but I procrastinated — even after writing down that same day a commitment to start working work on it. Sound familiar? Have you ever faced this same challenge?

I did work on making a list of the 100 nuggets and had maybe 40 or 50 listed by May. But then I became very busy conducting one or two inspections per day and lost my focus on writing the book. Fortunately, during church in January 2015, the sermon by Pastor Kevin Myers was focused on "re-enlisting" and I knew that I needed to refocus my attention to the book.

So, as one who has a weakness of not being able to stay on task, perhaps your tactics for staying on task serve you better than my tactics. However, I will list below what I feel are tactics that can help those weak in this area of staying on task and those with a proficiency in this. Some of the tactics I utilize are:

1. Writing down a list of 5 to 10 items to work on the next day.

2. Carrying over from the previous day's list to the subsequent day's list any items not completed.

3. Pray that God will show me the important things for me to work on that day when I say my morning prayers.

4. Using my wife or one of my children as a sounding board or accountability partner to keep me focused on what I have told them I must get done. (I think this is a great practice to get your spouse or children involved in what is going on as a family or even important business tasks and to get them to feel a part of the process to help you.)

5. Once a month or more frequently compile a list of the bigger projects that need to get done in the future; at which point they will show up on the daily "To-Do List."

43. Hard Work Trumps Natural Ability

I am a graduate of Georgia Tech and once followed their football and basketball programs closely. In basketball it is easy to get a good understanding of the players because there are only five starters, and Georgia Tech typically only played eight or nine players in each game. So you could get to know those players fairly well.

In the 1990s, I was working for a small, private company, who sold their products to the poultry industry. One of the VPs of the company was telling me that he had gone to a high school basketball gym where two local Atlanta basketball teams were playing.

He was watching before the game, when a small sparrow flew through the gym toward a Georgia Tech player, who happened to be standing near the doorway. He watched in amazement as this bird flew towards this player and the player quickly stuck out his hand and caught the bird in midair. Obviously, this made a memorable impression on the VP of our company. So the next time he saw me at work, he made a point of retelling the story.

The Vice President knew this Georgia Tech player was a heralded recruit, and was one of the stars of the Tech basketball. He recanted the story to me and went on to say that he thought this player would have a long career in the NBA.

I had seen several Tech games in the "Thriller Dome" that year and watched many more games on TV, and I was even more impressed with another player on the team. This player was not as heralded but was a top player, and hustled more than any other person on the team.

When the VP said he thought the player would have a long career in the NBA, my immediate response was that I thought this other player, who was more of a hustler, would turn out to be the better player over time. By the time they were both seniors, the player I identified as a better hustler was drafted in the first round of the NBA draft, while the player the VP identified as a better talent went undrafted.

This gold nugget affirms the biblical axiom, that God rewards hard work. This axiom is distributed throughout the Bible. Whatever we do, we should do it with all our might, with all our heart. And when we work with these things in mind, others, both Christians and non-Christians, will notice. Consider this verse from Proverbs 10:4, "Lazy hands make a man poor, but diligent hands bring wealth."

Also from Colossians 3:23-24:"Whatever you do, work at it with all your heart, as working for the Lord, not for men, since you know that you will receive an inheritance from the Lord as a reward. It is the Lord Christ you are serving."

Therefore, in all that we do, let us do it with purpose, knowing that God rewards hard work, and that hard work can trump natural ability.

44. Develop a Daily Routine

Do you have a prayer time? Do you have a time each day set aside to read the Bible? What about meditation time? Oh and don't forget about your paying job? And also the kids; remember you want to get your quality time in with them. And don't forget to make time for a weekly date night. It sounds like a busy life doesn't it? Yes, we all lead very busy lives.

Matthew 6:21 reminds us: "For where your treasure is, there your heart will be also." These words admonish us to find time in our life for those things we treasure the most. We all know this is true, that we push off to the corners of our life the things that are less important, but Jesus wants our heart to treasure Him.

God tells us in Jeremiah 29:13: "You will seek me and find me when you seek me with all of your heart." I have shared with you how I turned my life over to Christ and how I have had a burning desire to know Jesus deeper and fuller since that day in December 2003.

Jesus put a thirst in my soul for the Word, and I have desired to seek Him with all of my heart since then. I have grown in my faith and in my spiritual maturity, and want to share with you some of the strategies as suggestions to deepen your walk with Jesus. Please weigh on your heart which of these resonates with you and perhaps you may come up with a routine to enrich your walk with Jesus.

Overall, I think the most important thing in seeking to deepen your spiritual life is to come up with a routine. While you may not be able to stick with the routine or schedule every day due to other appointments, having a base to come back to and move from that is familiar will assist you in sticking with your game plan.

Most Christians would agree that setting time aside for your spiritual growth is best done in the morning. Many people make this time the first thing in the morning. If you are a morning person this will probably resonate with you. I prefer to have my time with the Lord in the morning, but I also have found it easier in our household to wake up and get my children out of the house to school. Then, once that rush of activity has subsided, I seek my quiet time with the Lord.

At this point, I want to share that most of my morning spiritual routine follows that of my senior pastor, Kevin Myers, of 12 Stone Church in Lawrenceville. He has used this routine called "praying around the diamond (or bases)" for over a decade. He also wrote a book on it, co-authored with John C. Maxwell, titled *Home Run* published in 2014 by Hachette Book Group, which I would encourage you to purchase.

Pastor Kevin, as we call him at 12 Stone, says "To love the Lord with all your heart is the second priority in prayer. The first priority in prayer is to fix ourselves." I find this quite insightful, that although we are striving to grow closer to God, it is us that are broken, and that to get closer to God, we must fix ourselves first.

Pastor Kevin suggests playing Christian songs as a first step in "praying around the bases." These songs are typically praise-and-worship songs that affirm and celebrate who God is.

I find getting my journal out before starting and writing down the names of two songs I feel are appropriate for the day works best for me. Sometimes the songs are combative songs, which take the offensive if I am feeling an unusual spiritual attack, but most days I just play two praise-and-worship songs.

I go to YouTube and select a video to watch of the songs but I understand most will prefer to listen to Spotify, Apple music or similar methods. I also find picking one of the videos which has the lyrics displayed during the showing of the video is helpful for me in solidifying what the vocalist is trying to convey in the song. After watching the videos, I either start declaring who God is (an awesome God, a mighty warrior, King of Kings, etc.) or go directly into thanking God for who He is, what He has done, and answered prayers.

The next part of Pastor Kevin's routine is first base, where you confess your sins. In this step, you speak (or better yet write down) known sin, and then write over these sins "Forgiven." This also is an appropriate time to ask God to reveal to you any sin you may not be aware of, and to bring that to your attention. If God brings something into focus, write it down and confess it, and write "Forgiven" over it.

The next part of the routine is to read the Bible and look for any link in what you read to what is going on in your life. Look for where you can glean wisdom from the reading to provide direction in your life. If there is nothing that stands out from that day's reading, don't worry. Because as you read the Bible each day, you are gaining wisdom which you will refer to in the future in discerning what God's will is for you.

The next step is second base, where you forgive others and pray for others, and seek His wisdom in all relationships, to assist you in finding peace with those around you. In this step you also seek to love others.

As Pastor Kevin states, "The greatest evidence that the love of God is in you is that you love others." I often pause after this step of praying for others to meditate and reflect.

Occasionally during this time, as I try to open my mind to whatever God would have me think of, I will think of someone I should pray for, or something I sense God is telling me to do. I write this down in my journal, along with my other journal notes for the day. This is the time I find God "speaks to me" or gives me direction.

The final step in "praying around the bases" is third base, where you pray through your work goals and pressures. This is where you seek God's wisdom for your work activities and ask for His favor in all of your work.

I find it important when doing this to talk to God as if He were your earthly Father, and as if your earthly Dad had asked you how things are going at work. Here is where you can pour out to our Wonderful Counselor all the pressure you are feeling and turn it over to Him. Ask for His direction as to what He would have you to do in your business decisions and career, just like you would if you were interviewing for a job and you were seeking His guidance as to whether you should take the job or not.

Finally, take it back to home plate by declaring you want all of your work to be done for the glory of God. Pastor Kevin suggests concluding this step with the Lord's Prayer, with a few words added in. After "on earth as it is in heaven," Pastor Kevin adds, "In this day, I commit to walk with You. I depend upon You to give me wisdom, strength, and favor as Your will is done in my life this day." I like the added words, that in speaking them we convey our commitment and dependence on God that day and ask for His wisdom, strength, and favor for that day.

This is one daily routine. You could modify it, or do one part one day and another part the next, or use another routine. But the important part is to have a routine, to have something you repeat over and over to honor and worship God. That is what God asked the Israelites to do; to come to the temple to honor Him. We do well to honor him daily and establish a daily routine that facilitates that specifically for us.

I hope this provides some stimulus for you to get in the game or step up your game if you are feeling your spiritual life is a little lacking. I sensed my spiritual life wasn't where God wanted it long before I turned my life over to God, when I was transitioning from a corporate job to starting up a home inspection company.

Therefore met with a life coach and, as part of the coaching, I told her I wanted to spend more time focused on spiritual things. God has led me to grow each year as a result of my seeking Him, and I pray He will for you also as you seek Him. It will probably take a while, if you are like me.

But remember Jeremiah 29:13 provides these reassuring words: "You will seek me and find me when you seek me with all of your heart."

45. Notes for Your Kids

When my wife was a child, her Dad used to put notes of encouragement in her lunches that she took to school. My Mom had four boys in five and a half years, perhaps, this is why in our house we did not make lunches the night before. We just bought the school lunches. But when our kids were young, my wife or I would write notes to them which were put in their lunches — not every day but on a regular basis.

We strive to support our kids and attend their sports games, their ballet recitals, and or whatever activities they are involved in. Our children love to hear and see our support of their activities.

It takes time, but we realize this is quality time where we bond as a family. During the time when we drove them to an activity, as we watched and cheered them on, and then as we transported them back home, we were doing an amazing thing: supporting and encouraging our children.

We would take time to put short notes of support in their lunches as another tangible way of letting them know they were being thought of during the day. Some of our encouragement came with us knowing it would be needed perhaps on a day when they received a low test score or if someone was mean to them. Opening a note of encouragement from us to them may have been just the boost or lift they need to help get through another day of school.

When our oldest child was a junior in high school, she befriended a classmate who was not experiencing a healthy home life, and his grades were suffering. As she became better friends with this young man, she introduced him to my wife and me.

After learning that he was often sleeping at friends' houses on their sofas, we offered that he could live with us for the rest of his junior and senior years if he wanted. He took us up on this offer, and we saw a steady improvement in his grades.

During this period of time, I began printing out Scripture verses into strips and putting them in my children's lunches and in this young man's lunches. He had started attending our church while living with us, and the Scripture verses served as another opportunity to fill him with God's Word and encouragement five days a week in addition to Sunday.

This could be a perfect spin on the standard note in the lunch that you may decide to do — or you may decide to do both. Either way, your children will appreciate and look forward to these "surprises." They may look forward in anticipation to seeing what note you sent them or what Scripture you included, so much so that when opening their lunch, they may first reach for the note and then for the food!

46. Songs for Your Daily Routine

In a previous gold nugget I suggested playing songs on your cell phone via a YouTube video as a great way to begin your daily spiritual routine. I have been doing this for about five years now and definitely can be motivated (even early in the morning) by listening to the Christian music.

My hope is you might benefit from my research on this music if you are not already incorporating music into your daily spiritual routine. Therefore, I thought I would share with you music I have found that works well for me and you can see if you like it.

I mentioned that most of the time I select two praise-and-worship songs to play, after first contemplating what songs I feel would be appropriate for that day. I keep a list of these songs and look over them to see which two resonate with my soul that day. There are literally thousands of these songs from hundreds of groups.

I don't want to limit the number of these songs, but will instead let you experiment on YouTube or Spotify to discover which particular ones you might like. But I can list many of the artists that are popular or that I like. Some of these are Hillsong, Jesus Culture, Chris Tomlin, Christy Nockels, Laura Story, Aaron Shust, Michael W. Smith, Matt Redman, Gateway Worship, Elevation Worship, John Waller, Misty Edwards, Cory Asbury, Nate Sallie, Nicol Sponberg, Kutless, Matthew West, Casting Crowns, Building 429, Tenth Avenue North, Planetshakers, Natalie Grant, Third Day, Newsboys, Chris August, and Lauren Daigle. These are just a few of the top Christian artists, but if you start with this list, you will find other similar artists and praise songs that might speak to you.

There are a limited number of songs that I have found to be particularly powerful in combating the enemy in spiritual warfare. So, as I mentioned, I play one or two of these songs on those days that I want to push into my head the fact that Satan is a defeated foe. I find playing these songs especially helpful to solidify that the enemy needs to leave me alone and that all I need is Jesus, and to fix my eyes, ears, and heart on Him.

Here is this short list of songs I use, with the corresponding artist.

1. "Our God Reigns Here" by John Waller Copyright ℗ 2009 Provident Label Group LLC, a division of Sony Music Entertainment

2. "Break Every Chain" by Jesus Culture Copyright ℗ 2011 Jesus Culture Music under exclusive license to Sparrow Records © 2015 Jesus Culture Music under exclusive license to Sparrow Records

3. "Stay Strong" by Newsboys Copyright ℗ Compilation 2007 Sparrow Records © 2007 Sparrow Records

4. "Good Fight" by Unspoken Copyright ℗ © 2014 Centricity Music

5. "Battle" by Chris August Copyright 2010 Word Music, LLC(Admin. by WB Music Corp.)

6. "Pressing On" by Kelanie Gloeckler Copyright © 2010 Kelanie Gloeckler

7. "Worship the Great I Am" by Gateway Worship Copyright © 2012 Walker Beach

8. "Our God" by Chris Tomlin Copyright ℗ © 2010 sixstepsrecords/ Sparrow Records

9. "Same Power" by Jeremy Camp Copyright ℗ © 2015 Stolen Pride Records LLC

10. "Fear Is a Liar" by Zach Williams Copyright ℗ 2016 Provident Label Group LLC, a division of Sony Music Entertainment

11. "No Longer Slaves" by Bethel Music Copyright © 2014 Bethel Music Publishing (ASCAP)

12. "Hello My Name Is" by Matthew West Copyright © 2012 Sparrow Records

47. If at First You Do Not Succeed, Try Again

If you set goals frequently, eventually there will come a time when a goal you have set will not be met. How will you react? What will you do when you don't reach your goal? Perhaps we should look for some insight from the most accomplished individuals in their area of expertise.

Michael Jordan, widely acclaimed as the greatest basketball player of all time, had to wait 7 years after being drafted to reach his 1st NBA championship with the Chicago Bulls. He states that on 26 occasions he was given the basketball to make the final winning shot and failed. He also states that over the course of his career, he missed almost 9000 shots.

To Jordan's credit he says, "I have failed over and over and over again in my life. And that is why I succeed." Or consider Abraham Lincoln's story. He was defeated twice in his bid to become an Illinois senator and once in seeking to be nominated for Vice President of the United States before being elected President of the United States in 1860.[4]

Undoubtedly, we will all fail at something in life (or many things in life), but that failure can be the springboard to reaching and attaining the goal or the success we desire. We can take inspiration from one of the icons of the New Testament —Peter. Remember that before His arrest Jesus told Peter, "Before the rooster crows you will deny me three times."

Peter replied, that he would never deny Jesus, but he did. But did that prevent Peter from accomplishing all that Jesus had planned for him? Not at all. Jesus said that "Peter was the rock upon which the church would be built."

Even though Peter had denied knowing Jesus three times, he was a central figure in the rapid spread of Christianity after Jesus' death. He was

---

4. Internet, Famous Failures, Michael Jordan, Abraham Lincoln and More — sidsavara. com/.../famous-failures-michael…

inspired by the Holy Spirit to speak to the crowd gathered on Pentecost and that day 3000 were baptized and became Christians. So, in our failures let us take inspiration from Michael Jordan, Abraham Lincoln and Peter. Let's run the race that God has placed us in with vigor and persistence.

48. Take Charge of Your Medical Records

We all know that more work is being required of doctors with more and more documentation. Just like in the business community, generally medical companies and hospitals are requiring more of their employees. I've experienced this when I took my mom for her monthly oncology appointments.

I understand the difficulty the doctors have when they need to act quickly, glancing at their patient's medical records' chart, and trying to remember everything that has transpired, relating to their condition. As I observed this dilemma, I decided to record the significant events in my mother's treatment for cancer.

So, I just typed up a Word document with the date of an action in the left column and then a description in the right column. I wrote the date my mom started her hormone therapy pills and the date she started her radiation treatment. After doing this for several months, the benefit of my efforts became clear when a specific date was required during a discussion with the oncologist.

I referred to my chart and quickly determined how many weeks it had been since she started a particular medication. The doctor commented that it was a good idea to chronicle the history of her cancer treatment. I recommend you begin to document your family's health history, especially when your children are young.

A quick note typed into a record for each family member may reveal illnesses that occur over-and-over such as ear infections in your children. It will help you to know how many times a particular illness is occurring, per year. It is a reliable way to take control of your medical information, so you will quickly be able to see what has transpired in your family's health history.

49. Don't Be a Naysayer

My mom was a great student of God's Word and a strong Christian. She often used the phrase, "Don't be a doubting Thomas." By this she was referring to the apostle Thomas. When the other disciples told him that Jesus had risen from the grave, Thomas said, "Unless I see the nail marks in His hands and put my hand into His side, I will not believe." When Jesus finally appeared to Thomas, He said, "Put your finger here; see my hands. Reach out your hand and put it into my side. Stop doubting and believe" (John 20:27).

It is obvious in looking at Jesus' life and listening to His words (spoken to the disciples and all those around Him) that believing was paramount. Not just the idea of faith, but believing in the signs and wonders that occurred around Jesus' life. In this verse Jesus is commanding Thomas to stop doubting and believe. Matthew 13:13-15 reads, "This is why I speak to them in parables: 'Though seeing, they do not see; though hearing, they do not hear or understand. In them is fulfilled the prophecy of Isaiah: 'You will be ever hearing but never understanding; you will be ever seeing but never perceiving. For this people's heart has become calloused; they hardly hear with their ears, and they have closed their eyes. Otherwise they might see with their eyes, hear with their ears, understand with their hearts and turn, and I would heal them.'"

I believe Jesus would rather us be naïve and innocent than closeminded and hardheaded. I believe Jesus would not want us to be a naysayer, but rather to believe in the signs and wonder and power of an Almighty God who is at work in our world—and will do even greater things if we will only believe. Remember what Jesus said in Matthew 18:2-5? "He [Jesus] called a little child and had him stand among them. And he said: 'I tell you the truth, unless you change and become like little children, you will never enter the kingdom of heaven. Therefore, whoever humbles himself like this child is the greatest in the kingdom of heaven. And whoever welcomes a little child like this in my name welcomes me." I believe Jesus wants us to believe like the centurion who had a sick servant. This is recorded in several of the Gospels, but here are the words from the Apostle Luke,

> "When Jesus had finished saying all this in the hearing of the people, he entered Capernaum. There a centurion's servant, whom his master valued highly, was sick and about to die. The centurion heard of Jesus and sent some elders of the Jews to him, asking him to come and heal his servant. When they came to Jesus, they pleaded earnestly with him, 'This man deserves to have you do this, because he loves our nation and has built our synagogue.' So Jesus went with them. He was not far from the house when the centurion sent friends to say to him: 'Lord, don't trouble yourself, for I do not deserve to have you come under my roof. That is why I did not even consider myself worthy to come to you. But say the word, and my servant will be healed. For I, myself, am a man under authority, with soldiers under me. I tell this one, 'Go,' and he goes; and that one, 'Come,' and he comes. I say to my servant, 'Do this,' and he does it.' When Jesus heard this, he was amazed at him, and turning to the crowd following him, he said, 'I tell you, I have not found such great faith even in Israel.' Then the men who had been sent returned to the house and found the servant well." (Luke 7:1-9).

There are many more stories from the Bible of how believing, or faith is what Jesus wanted from those around Him, and He wants the same from us today. Atheists are naysayers, agnostics are naysayers and many of the highly educated that put all their faith in their own knowledge are naysayers. But we as Christians should not be naysayers. We should be like children which are innocent and naïve—if you tell them something, they believe you. So be like children and believe, and as my mom would say, "Don't be a doubting Thomas."

Gold Nuggets to
Experience God

50. Schedule Encounters with God

Do you mean you can plan encounters with God? Well, not exactly. But you can certainly increase the likelihood that God will show up if you schedule consistent times to spend with God, to seek Him.

On our wall in our kitchen is an idiom:

> "Make time for the quiet moments as God whispers and
> the world is loud."

I think that sums up the philosophy behind this gold nugget. It is hard to find God if your life is so busy with daily activities that you only leave a sliver of time in which to connect with God. The [Old Testament or Bible] says that the Sabbath is God's and we should not work on that day. But I think in practice we do not set the whole day aside for God but rather feel content in worshiping at church for an hour or so on Sundays.

So how do we create an environment where we can really connect with God, where we really encounter God's Spirit? About five years ago, I joined a father-son small group at our church. Those who know me probably wondered, "Wait, Daniel, you don't have any sons." And they were right.

I have three daughters and no sons. But the small-group leader set it up in a Saturday morning small group setting to involve fathers, with an occasional overnight father-son trip into the mountains of North Georgia, where his father had a large cabin. He was happy to have me join the camping trips.

Most of the camping trips ended up with simply the Dads going. It was during these times that we intentionally sought God. I found the trips to be very gratifying, peaceful, and renewing.

The men would pray over one another and talk about things going on in their lives. Because we were in the mountains, we often did not have a cell phone signal. So we were not distracted and could really connect with one another and with God.

It reminds me of the way that Jesus Christ would pull away from the disciples to get some quiet time to pray. I developed a respect for seeking quiet moments when God might whisper to me – and when I was able to hear God's whisper, which otherwise might have passed by me unheard.

So, whether you plan time away from your hectic life with your church group, family or simply by yourself, also do plan time in your schedule to be with God, and to be quiet and open as He speaks to you.

51. Be Bold

I want to preface this gold nugget by distinguishing that there is a difference, particularly in a biblical context, between being bold and with being proud. The concept of being humble is distributed throughout the Bible as a virtue whereas the concept of being proud is admonished throughout the Bible.

Pride is not a virtue, but being bold, at the appropriate time, is commendable. In being confident, we are to be bold at the things that are of God or that He has placed on our hearts or led us to do.

There are several places in the Bible where we see a person being bold and strong in the Lord. I believe these examples serve as learning experiences for each one of us. In Genesis 18, Abraham is talking with God about His plans to destroy the cities of the Sodom and Gomorrah:

> "Then Abraham spoke up again: 'Now that I have been so bold as to speak to the Lord, though I am nothing but dust and ashes, what if the number of the righteous is five less than fifty? Will you destroy the whole city because of five people?'" (Genesis 18:27-28)

So Abraham is bold enough to first ask God not to destroy the city if there are 50 righteous people in the cities, and then he reduces the number to 45, then to 40, then to 30, then to 20. Finally he stops pleading when God says He will agree not to destroy the city if 10 righteous people are found. It seems that Abraham is negotiating with the God of the Universe over God's plans. But we know God is sovereign and He had a plan already in mind. Still God honored Abraham's boldness and granted each subsequent plea.

In my opinion God granted his requests because Abraham was pursuing Godly virtues; that is, not wishing any righteous people to perish. So we see here that if our desires or intentions are in line with God's will that God will honor our boldness in pursuing them.

Of course, the story of David and Goliath loudly proclaims the boldness of David, even at the young age of 15. Goliath, who was a Philistine giant about nine or ten-feet tall, had intimidated the Israeli army for 40 days.

The story is recounted in 1st Samuel 17. David, who was not with the Israeli army, was watching the flock of sheep for his father Jesse, who ended up asking David to take 10 loaves of bread and an ephah of roasted grain to his brothers on the battle line.

When David heard Goliath challenging the Israelis, he approached King Saul and asked that he let him battle Goliath. Saul told David he was just a boy and would not be able to go out against Goliath. But David persisted, and told Saul that he had had killed lions and bears when they attacked his father's sheep. So Saul relented, and David went out to battle Goliath. Before slaying him, 1st Samuel 17:45-47 tells us: "David said to the Philistine, 'You come against me with sword and spear and javelin, but I come against you in the name of the Lord Almighty, the God of the armies of Israel, whom you have defied. This day the Lord will hand you over to me, and I'll strike you down and cut off your head. Today I will give the carcasses of the Philistine army to the birds of the air and the beasts of the earth, and the whole world will know that there is a God in Israel. All those gathered here will know that it is not by sword or spear that the Lord saves; for the battle is the Lord's, and he will give all of you into our hands.'"

So David, using a stone and a sling, killed Goliath. This is holy boldness! First, even after his oldest brother's reprimand, David is bold enough to approach King Saul for permission to fight Goliath.

Secondly, he doesn't change his approach even after he is turned down the first time. Instead, he continues with his request until the king says yes. Then, upon entering the battlefield and approaching Goliath, he boldly proclaimed in the face of this giant that he will kill him this very day. So, again, we see that because he was doing the will of God and had faith in God, he could act boldly, and God delivered Goliath into his hands.

I think it no coincidence that both of these stories are some of the most widely-known of the Bible. They both demonstrate that, when doing what God would have us to do, we can be bold. They demonstrate that we don't need to be timid, that He is the source of our strength, and that we can and should have an inner confidence and peace like David did when we are undertaking the work of the Lord. May God grant us the wisdom to know when to step up for the Lord, and when to do it boldly.

52. Be Filled With the Holy Spirit

It goes without saying that as Christians we all want to be filled with the Holy Spirit. We all want to live for Him and be filled with joy for Him and joy for life. And when we are born again, God does give us a new life, the old is cast out and the Holy Spirit enters us and begins a new work in us.

But generally, in order to be filled with the Spirit and to be filled with joy, we have to get rid of everything that holds us back and everything that hinders us from attaining the life God wants for us. It is like cleaning out a closet. We must remove everything that is old to make room for the new. In order to fit new stuff into a cluttered and cramped closet, we must do a "spring cleaning."

It is key when we are born again to take the time to dwell on our past and sincerely want to repent of our sins, and turn from those things. In so doing we can break free from those things that were of the former self to make room for the new joy, peace, and other qualities that the Holy Spirit wants to fill us with. Many Christians seem to be stuck at a certain point in life rather than growing in their spirituality and living a richer, fuller life.

God has been showing me that for us to grow spiritually and live an abundant life, we must go back and get rid of anything that hinders that from our past. This means being willing to repent and sincerely ask Him to forgive us for the things we did in the past that we know were not of God.

We need to pray and ask Him to bring to our attention anything that we have not repented of and immediately confess these sins. God, who is faithful and just, will forgive us our sins and cleanse us from all unrighteousness. (1 John 1:9)

Many people have a problem with God completely forgiving them. They think that what they have done in the past is too bad and God wants to punish them for it. There is punishment for sin and it is the atoning work of Jesus Christ that overcomes our sins. For those who repent and are truly sorry for their sins, and lay them on the altar for God to deal

137

with, He does forgive. It isn't necessary to ask for forgiveness again in the future. It is done and finished the first time you take it to God and repent of it. So believe that and break free from your past and live in the new life that God wants for you.

I encourage you to not take your past nonchalantly. Do not assume that because you accepted Christ as your personal Savior that you never need to repent of sins. Yes the prior sins are wiped clean by the blood of Jesus when we accept Christ. But we are still going to sin moving forward and those sins should be repented of whenever you are aware of them. Also the enemy has a way of reminding us of our previous sins through guilt and condemnation. While God has forgiven your former sins when you accept Christ, you may also need to forgive yourself. For many people this helps bring closure on their former sins that God has already forgiven so that they may move forward to new places in their faith.

We should take all things to God in prayer, especially things that are troubling us (which may be Satan's work), and things which you feel God is bringing up to you so that you will repent of them. Generally there are many things from our past that tend to bring our spirits down, and if we ask God to help us with these things, He will.

53. Express Your Love for God

Randall Grier, who has a worldwide ministry, states that the best way to express your love for God is to keep His commandments. God gave Moses the Ten Commandments for His people to live their life by, and if we do love God, we should seek to please Him in addition to fearing him by keeping His commandments.

The Ten Commandments were given for our good, because God loves us, because He knows that without them we succumb easily to the tactics and ploys of the Enemy. In this respect, good earthly fathers, who want to protect their children, are like God. Rules protect and provide clear guidance for us.

For example, a loving father would tell his children to stay away from the edge of the Grand Canyon. The father knows one of his responsibilities is to protect his children because he loves them. He institutes rules so they don't get hurt. In the same way, listening and obeying are ways for earthly children to show their love for their earthly father. So it is the same for us as we follow our Heavenly Father and obey His commandments.

Since God loved us so much that He gave His only Son to die for us, we should love God back. One of the best ways to show Him we love Him is by keeping His commandments. Randall Grier states, "God gave us the commandments because He loved us and wanted to bless us."

Many people think that rules are meant to constrain or limit us; but in fact, rules give us liberty and are a blessing to us. Think of a young child who is told by his father or mother never to step off of the curb and into the street, where a car could hit him.

Is that rule or boundary on the part of the parent an act of love to keep them alive and or is it a punishment? As it relates to the Ten Commandments, God's view of liberty is freedom from sin and its substantial consequences. The apostle John understood that the best way to love God is to keep His commandments for he stated in 1st John 5:3 that "This is love for God: to obey his commands. And his commands are not burdensome."

Paul also grasped this as he wrote in 1 Corinthians 7:19, "Circumcision is nothing and uncircumcision is nothing. Keeping God's commands is what counts." In essence what Paul is stating is being circumcised doesn't matter, but what does matter is keeping God's commands. If we love God and want to express our love to Him in response to His love for us, we should keep His commandments.

I have a friend I talk to on the phone quite often and he will conclude his conversation with, "I love you." Do I respond with something blasé like "I'll talk with you later"? No, I want to reciprocate his expression of love for me. Accordingly, I respond with, "Love you back" or "Love you too." So if God loved us by giving us the Ten Commandments to keep us from sin and the terrible consequences that come along with sin, our ultimate act of loving God back should be to keep the Ten Commandments.

54. God's Will

Have you ever felt God impress on you to undertake a certain task or do a certain thing? Not many people actually hear God speak to them and tell them exactly what to do, but many people feel a gentle nudge or get a thought of what the Lord is leading them to do.

My advice is to pray and take the steps to do what He is leading you to do. There are many seasons in life, and God may change his direction for you in the future. He may want you to do something different. So, you may need to stop what you felt He told you to do previously.

We call this "doing the next right thing." In doing this, you follow God's lead, while realizing you are on a journey, and the path He has for you may change in the future.

A circumstance where this played out in my professional life occurred several years ago. I had been a home inspector for many years, and was still spending two to three hours after work at home typing up reports for each home inspection that I conducted.

If I had two inspections in one day, each typically taking three hours to conduct plus the drive time, then I was looking at about a 15 or 16 hour workday. I joined a group of home inspectors that shared information with each other on how to improve various aspects of your home inspection business.

Using the techniques I learned as part of this group I was able to decrease my time of typing inspection reports to about one hour per inspection, which gave me more time with my family in the evenings.

Additionally, I believe God also led me to join this group to put me in touch with a publicist to assist me with the writing and representation of this book. This occurred at the group's annual convention, when the publicist was invited to speak on how to increase publicity for our home inspection businesses.

God used this contact to get the ball rolling on my book. Then, although the inspection group's purpose was to facilitate greater efficiency and revenue in our home inspection businesses, I felt God leading me to direct more of my time on spiritual issues rather than on the home-inspection business.

So, although I had learned a lot from this group and grown my business, I felt led to discontinue my membership in this group. Within a month after stopping my membership, God reunited me with an old friend, who I began mentoring.

God originally led me to join the inspection group for two specific reasons, after these purposes had been fulfilled, He led me to discontinue membership in this group. And when I followed what I felt were His promptings, he confirmed my thought that He wanted to use me in more spiritual areas by having me begin mentoring this former friend.

The way I sensed He was leading me in this other direction was I felt dissatisfied working all the time and not having time for the spiritual things which I longed to spend more time on. I felt an uneasiness in my spirit, and I pondered this and prayed about it.

God's response was to lead me to do less rather than more in my home inspection business. There is always the question of how to know God's will. My hope is this story, of how God worked in this situation in my life, will provide some direction or insight for you.

If you struggle with a certain decision or you feel as if your life is not heading in the right direction, stop and ask God to make His way clear to you. He has promised to hear us when we call out to Him and He also has promised to lead and guide us through each day.

55. Soar to New Heights

What do you want? Do you desire deep unfathomable joy? Do you desire to feel how much God loves you? Do you want the peace that passes all human understanding in your life? Do you know there is a way to obtain all of these things?

Many people experience life to the full, and God wants us all to experience it. When we surrender completely to God and submit to His will for us—where we are living inside His good and perfect will instead of within our faulty desires and wishes—that is when we hit the sweet spot, the spot that is called "life to the full" in John 10:10.

God's will is perfect. His ways are perfect. And when we make the focus of our lives to please Him each and every day by doing His will, He will pour out blessings into our lives beyond what we can imagine.

When we focus on others instead of ourselves, God uses that for His glory and pours out blessings into our life along the way. I believe the key is to change our perspective from "What can I do to improve my life" to "What can I do for others that will bless them and enrich their lives?"

When we go out of our way to help others they will sense it; they will recognize the kindness, and they will be touched by it. They may be in a rough place in life and put up a wall or have a hardened heart, but when you do the unexpected, when you show a random act of kindness it will melt away a small portion of that hardened heart.

This might provide all the opening that God needs to come into their life—all because you acted like Christ and did something for them they did not ask for. Their proverbial "door" might have been closed and by your action it may be cracked open a bit. That opening may be exactly what God was looking for someone to do, and He may send the Holy Spirit through that opening to blow the door wide open and let the winds of the Holy Spirit swirl around and bring about change in their life.

That is what it is all about—changing lives for Christ, one by one. When Jesus walked on this earth, that is what He did; one by one Jesus served people. You will find that people can tell when you really care about them, when your focus is on blessing them and helping them anyway you can. This is God's will—for us to be a blessing to others, to surrender to our own desires and let God's desires shine through us—He will pour out blessings into our lives.

There is no greater feeling than knowing without a doubt that you are right in the middle of God's will, doing what He would have you to do. When you help someone in their time of need, when they were down and out, you lead them to a richer, fuller life in Christ.

It is so fulfilling when you know that God led you specifically to this person during their darkest hour. And when they respond positively, there is joy—to know that you are doing exactly what God wanted you to do. And when they turn to God because He used you to accomplish His will, you come to realize that you didn't just help them (through God's strength) to experience a change in their life, but they were snatched from the jaws of the Enemy so they could experience eternal life with God.

That is where the joy and peace of God comes from, when you know you are doing exactly what God would have you to do at that particular moment. And because you were obedient, He used you to eternally change the life of another. It just doesn't get much better than that.

Suggested Prayer:

Father, in the name of Jesus who served this fallen world, help me to be like Jesus and put the needs of this world above my needs and desires. Help me to desire the things of your world above the things of this world. Help me to die daily to my desires just as Jesus died daily to worldly desires and died on the cross for all humanity.

Fill me with your Spirit so that I might have the heart of Jesus, seeking to save others and bring them into the fullness of the life that is in Christ Jesus. Reveal to me and then empower me at the appropriate time to assist those that you would have me minister to. Help me to be a friend of sinners like Jesus, not judging or condemning, and live with abandon doing random acts of kindness. And Father, as I do this fill me with an even greater measure of Your love, and saturate my soul with the joy of life that is ours in Christ Jesus.

56. God's Timing Is Perfect

Have you ever noticed how God's timing is perfect? Have you ever looked back in hindsight on a sequence of events and realized just how He orchestrated everything and put it all together. I believe that God does this with each of us; that if we could see the spiritual realm, He is working for our favor to connect us to the proper people at the proper time. I think most of the time it passes right by us without us even becoming aware of it. But God's timing is perfect.

This was true in Biblical times and it is true now. Think about the story of Lazarus told in the John 11. Jesus frequently stayed with this family of beloved friends, which included Mary (who poured the expensive perfume on Jesus' feet and wiped it with her hair), Martha, and Lazarus. They lived in Bethany.

When Lazarus became extremely sick, his sisters sent word to Jesus asking that Jesus come and heal him. But when Jesus received their message, He stayed where he was and did not hurry to them. By the time He did arrive to their home, Lazarus had passed away.

In fact, he had been dead for four days. Many believe the Savior waited, not only to show his power to raise the dead to life, by which the Jewish leaders might say Jesus simply revived Lazarus' spirit. At this time Jewish leaders felt that your spirit departed you once you had been dead for three days, and for Jesus to raise Lazarus from the dead after four days would be a more emphatic proclamation of His power.

For Mary and Martha, 'perfect timing' would have been for Jesus to arrive and heal Lazarus before he passed. But in Jesus' perfect timing He knew an even greater miracle would be to raise Lazarus from the dead after four days, serving God's purpose in an even greater way.

Many times in our own life we think this or that should happen at a certain point. But God is in control, and it doesn't always work out that way. He can use His perfect timing for His purpose, which is usually beyond our comprehension. As it says in Isaiah 55:8: "For my thoughts are not your thoughts, neither are your ways my ways," declares the Lord.

There have been several times when I reflect back and see how God's timing was perfect in a situation in my life. One particular time was in the last six months of my mom's life, when her health was failing her due to cancer. Our oldest daughter was in college.

Mom had already contributed financially to help my wife and me with some of her college bills, but she had made no plans for helping fund the cost of college for our younger two daughters nor my brother's two children. While she had the financial means to assist us with their college funding, she had said when she was healthier she would consider assisting financially on a case-by-case basis with each child.

Then one night at the gym, I met a guy I believe God placed in my life for just this reason. You see, he was a financial planner. My wife and I met with him, but had already met with other financial planners, so we decided not to use his services.

In talking about this with my Mom, she started thinking about it and was inclined to set up accounts to help with all her grandchildren's college funding. So, this financial planner put us in touch with an attorney who specialized in establishing trusts specifically for this purpose.

We later learned this attorney had once worked as a junior attorney under the attorney, who assisted my wife and me in planning our estate, and had since retired. The junior attorney had gone on to start his own practice.

So, in my eyes, God orchestrated my chance encounter with this financial planner, who in turn put us in touch with his contact for an estate planning attorney. God stirred in my Mom's heart a desire to move forward and plan for a time when she would not be with us allowing us to set aside funds for my two other children, who were in high school and also for my brother's two children.

God was clearly working in all of this, and we were able to get the funding established, and get mom's signatures on it all while she was in good enough health to sign the papers. Yes God's timing and the sequence of events was perfect -- and my Mom felt very good that she had been moved to take care of this before she passed.

57. Do Not Love the World

Do not love the world or anything in the world. If anyone loves the world, the love for the Father is not in them. For everything in the world - the cravings of sinful man, the lust of his eyes, and the boasting of what he has and does - comes not from the Father but from the world. The world and its desires pass away, but the man who does the will of God lives forever. (1 John 2:15-17)

A high percentage of non-Christians love the world, embracing everything that the world presents to them without the discretion that comes from weighing things against the truth of the Bible. But we read in this verse in 1 John that these things of the world come not from God but from the enemy of our souls. But if we "do not love the world" and turn away from the worldly things to turn towards God, we will experience everlasting life.

So we should live a distinctively different life from non-Christians and not embrace the things that they do. Therefore, in a world where sex sells, Christians need to embrace modesty.

In a world where pornography is rampant, Christians should put blocks on their computers and telephones so that they cannot view pornography, even if tempted. When the world tells us "if it feels good, do it," Christians should abstain from sex before marriage and outside of marriage.

"The lust of the eyes" pertains to craving and accumulating material things. We all want more — more clothes, more toys, and a bigger and better house. These desires appear to be rampant in the U.S. now. And it appears when those from other countries come into the United States and become successful, they adopt our aspirations and way of life, even if it isn't that way in their country. But some do adhere to good biblical values and retain strong family traditions.

The third element of verse 16, "the boasting of what he has and does" refers to pride that comes from one's status or importance. This was one of my greatest failings before I was born again. I was relatively successful, moving up the corporate ladder, and I took pride in what I had accomplished.

At the time, I was not giving God the credit, but thinking, because I had done certain things that prove accomplishment in the business arena, that I had achieved these only through my hard work. I remember completing an exercise that a life coach sent to me which analyzed what your tendencies were towards. The exercise indicated that my so called "strength" was pride.

In many business circles, the thinking is that it's important to "toot your own horn" and be proud of what you have accomplished, and to make others aware of what you have accomplished by boasting is upheld. But God wants us to be humble, to be grateful for whatever we have, and to give Him the credit as He blesses us in our lives.

Notice how in writing this passage, John, after expressing three ways we can all fall into loving the world, concludes the passage. After he lists the three ways, he gives us the truth that we can all cling to, that give us the incentive or reward for turning away from this dark world — for it is not easy to do and many become ensnarled in it.

But he states that "the world and its desires pass away," but that the man who does the will of God lives forever. This flies contrary to a familiar bumper sticker which states "Whoever dies with the most toys wins," and instead leads us to dwell on the fact that "You can't take it with you."

The note for this verse in The Life Application Bible reads, "When our attachment to possessions is strong, it's hard to believe that what we want will one day pass away. It may be even harder to believe that the person who does the will of God will live forever." But as we loosen our grip on material things and focus on God living humble lives according to His will, we place ourselves in a position to experience the eternal life John refers to here.

58. Soar to New Heights II – Love Your Enemies

Do you really want to have God fill you with His Spirit and the fruit of the Spirit as listed in Galatians 5:22? Do you want to feel the power of God at work in your life? You can soar to new heights when you do the more radical things the average Christian doesn't contemplate, but which God may be calling you to do.

In Luke 6:27-36, Jesus is teaching His disciples to stop and think deeply about their lives as they connect with others: "But I tell you who hear me: Love your enemies, do good to those who hate you, bless those who curse you, pray for those who mistreat you. If someone strikes you on one cheek, turn to him the other also. If someone takes your cloak, do not stop him from taking your tunic. Give to everyone who asks you, and if anyone takes what belongs to you, do not demand it back. Do to others as you would have them do to you."

> "If you love those who love you, what credit is that to you? Even 'sinners' love those who love them. And if you do good to those who are good to you, what credit is that to you? Even 'sinners' do that. And if you lend to those from whom you expect repayment, what credit is that to you? Even 'sinners' lend to 'sinners', expecting to be repaid in full. But love your enemies, do good to them, and lend to them without expecting to get anything back. Then your reward will be great, and you will be sons of the Most High, because he is kind to the ungrateful and wicked. Be merciful, just as your Father is merciful."

Are these not radical words spoken by Jesus in Luke, chapter 6? These are not actions the typical Christian puts into play in their daily lives, but when reading these verses I think of people who give all for the kingdom of God —like Mother Theresa.

In my opinion, few in life can live to these standards, but the ones that do, do like Mother Theresa, probably experience joy like few others have, and that spurs them on to keep doing radical acts like these mentioned in this passage of Scripture. In our litigation-happy society here in America, the world tells you "to get all that you deserve." You are encouraged not to let anyone take advantage of you, and to exact revenge on anyone who harms you. But Jesus told us to "forgive our neighbors."

In these verses He is encouraging us to, "love your enemies, do good to those who hate you, and pray for those who mistreat you." Just think how much fewer divorces there would be if Christians lived out this principle. Just think how many attorneys would be put out of business for lack of work. Consider how many less murders there would be if others lived by these standards, which Christ calls us all to do.

In Luke 6:35 says, "Then your reward will be great, and you will be sons of the Most High, because he is kind to the ungrateful and wicked."

Our reward will not just be a "good" reward for doing good, but our reward will be "great." This seems rational, doesn't it? If we do good to those who harm us—like Jesus did in His passion when His detractors spit on Him and mocked Him—we will receive a great reward like Jesus did.

We know He is in Heaven, seated on the right hand of the Father, and this passage tells us we will be His children. Just as Jesus is His child, we too will share in the things of Heaven.

Suggested Prayer:

Father, we could never do the things You ask us to do in our own strength, for they are foreign to us and go against everything that this world teaches us. But through Jesus Christ's shed blood and death and on the cross, we can do all things. Therefore Father, in the name of Jesus, we ask You to make us like Your perfect Son who endured the cross and faced ridicule, even though He knew what would happen. He surrendered His will to Your will. Father, help us through the power of Your Son Jesus Christ to love those who hate us, to show love to those who take advantage of us, and to pray for those who mistreat us. For it is in the strength of Your Son, Jesus, that we can do all things.

59. Fix Anything

Have you ever noticed when someone knows every aspect of a machine they can always fix it? I have never taken my car in to be fixed and had the repair shop mechanic say, "We don't know how to fix your car."

It may be that the cost is prohibitive, but the mechanics can always figure out what needs to be done and repair your car so it runs properly. Or how about a copier repair technician who services a copy machine in an office? It seems that regardless of who the technician is and what the problem is, when you call about a copier repair they can always fix it.

It's because they know the machine inside out; they know when one part of the machine is not working the way it should be or is broken. The key to being able to fix anything is to completely know the ins and outs of whatever you are working on. Then I thought that is the ultimate goal for Christians: to know God completely so that we can draw on that knowledge and know what to do regardless of the situation we are faced with.

Of course, when we are intimately attached with Jesus He lives in us and helps us in whatever situation arises, and we can call on His supernatural power to help us. But on many occasions, there is not enough time to pray; something develops and we must make the best decision we can.

It is in these times, when we can draw on the wealth of knowledge that can be ours through knowing Scripture, being focused on God, and having the Holy Spirit with us to guide and direct us. If we can get to the point of knowing the Bible as well as a mechanic knows a car's engine, we will be able to handle life's situations more readily than with a life lived apart from God.

There is Scripture that deals with almost any conceivable issue; money, infidelity, greed, death, sickness and more. If we know the truth of God on these issues, (and memorize Scripture so it is quickly accessible), it will yield more confidence and peace when we're confronted by stressful situations.

I believe God would like all of us to be so grounded in His Word and so connected to Him that hardly anything would occur which would shake us off of our firm foundation in Him. That is what I mean by this title of "Fix Anything." I pray that you and your family will be able to handle anything because you continue to seek God and grow in knowledge of Him, day after day.

60. Tune In to the Holy Spirit

The Holy Spirit is probably the least talked about person in the Holy Trinity. We hear the expressions like "Jesus take the wheel" or "Let Go and Let God," but there is not a similar expression for the Holy Spirit. Not that this is a problem as they are all one, but I think if we actively seek the Holy Spirit like we talk about seeking God, we will be more mindful of how the Spirit is working in our lives.

We will become more passionate about our faith and responsive to how God is working through our life when we see more and more evidence of the Holy Spirit at work in our day-to-day lives. I believe what the Bible says when it describes a great outpouring of the Holy Spirit in the last days. There will be many signs and wonders that the Holy Spirit is much more active in the last days, so it seems fitting that we should become more familiar with these signs and get in touch with the Holy Spirit.

In the athletic world, the term "in the zone" refers to the state their minds—they are totally focused for the game. Likewise, for Christians I believe there are periods when the Holy Spirit is mightily present. Have you ever experienced one of these moments where perhaps you were praying in a group and the Holy Spirit just seemed to take over the prayer?

Suddenly, the most eloquent words just seemed to fly off of your tongue. That may well have been the inspiration of the Holy Spirit. He will give us thoughts, ideas, and words that are not our own, and if we are aware of this and recognize Him as the source, God can use it for great things in His kingdom.

Often God will bring something about that we will know was through the work of the Holy Spirit. Some describe it as "being moved by the Holy Spirit." For me, one of these times of being moved by the Holy Spirit came shortly after I awoke one Saturday morning. I took our dog on a leash out to the end of the driveway to get the morning paper.

As I did I observed my neighbor coming out of her house, letting her two dogs out. Although it was first thing in the morning, the thought immediately came into my head to phone her and invite her to our recently opened satellite church location. So I called her that afternoon, as prompted by the Holy Spirit.

We talked for about 15 minutes and she told me that she had been thinking of getting back into church and would love to try out our new location. So what the Holy Spirit did was connect me with her and her desire to resume attending a church. Other times the Holy Spirit will illuminate our minds and give us intuition into a situation that could not have been known—without the inspiration of the Holy Spirit.

An example of this was when my brother Ron was considering taking a job with a new company. He called me looking for insight from Lisa and me. When I asked Lisa about it, immediately she had a feeling that he should not take the job. I conveyed this to Ron and he decided not to take the job. Three months later he told Lisa and me that the company had gone out of business.

To be "dialed in" as a Christian, we need to be intentional and open to the promptings of the Holy Spirit. Many of us go through each day focused on the tasks at hand and doing them in our own strength with little time or room for the Holy Spirit to enter through our busy schedules. But if we schedule time each day for prayer and meditation, it opens us up to experience many great things that occur through the moving of the Holy Spirit.

We also must be willing to step out of our comfort zone and say "yes" to the promptings of the Holy Spirit—some of which may seem rather wacky to us as we step out of this world and into the workings of the spiritual realm. If you are open and willing, it may result in many awe-fulfilling experiences that will grow your faith and put you in better touch with the spiritual realm.

Gold Nuggets for Self-Improvement

61. Just Do It!

Many Christians read the Bible regularly and pray regularly. It may not be easy to find time in our busy schedules to do this, but if we put God first in our lives then we will make time to spend time in the Word and in prayer daily.

As I was doing research for this book, I read something in Philippians 4 that caught my eye. Paul, writes:

> "Whatever you have learned or received or heard from me, or seen in me - put it into practice. And the God of peace will be with you" (Philippians 4:9).

We can read the Bible. We can pray. We can go to church. But if we don't put what we learn in the Word or in church into practice, it doesn't amount to much. Paul was not boasting here; he had attained a spiritual stature in which he could be in prison and still sing songs of praise to God.

He gave God all the credit in verse 13 of this same chapter: "I can do everything through him who gives me strength."

He was telling us that God had developed him to be able to do all things, and God was the source of this inner strength that he possessed. Through this inner strength, Paul had an eternal sense of peace. This means he could be content and filled with joy even in prison.

So, for us, it is important to put into practice all that we have heard, learned, or that God has shown us. We will only grow by stretching ourselves, and changing ourselves, which comes not from reading but by doing – thereby, for Christians, we find a greater significance in the phrase, "Just do it!"

62. Have Compassion

Compassion is not a word that is used much in our world today, which makes sense because this world seems to be focused only on "me." With selfie photos, and the majority of people "looking out for number one," the focus in this society is not on others, but on "what's in it for me." If we reflect back on Christ's life and ministry, we see compassion lived out through Him to others. And, certainly if we stopped to think of "what would Jesus really do," we would become more compassionate, like Him.

Jesus was the ultimate example of compassion. When He was dying on the Cross after being flogged, spit on and having the Roman soldiers cast lots for His clothes, He said, "Forgive them Lord for they know not what they do" (Luke 23:24). This statement sets the bar pretty high. And if we think of this example when facing adversity or persecution, we realize that we have the ability to respond to wrongs done to us the way Christ did.

What is your first reaction? Is it to get mad at the perpetrator or to have compassion on them? Jesus taught us to pray for our enemies. This means that we take a moment to think through the situation and to give it to the Lord. When you are treated unfairly, pray for the perpetrators, who in essence are your enemies at the time.

At some point in life, we have all been wounded. We all need healing from previous hurts, and I believe that because many of us are in various places of hurt, our first reaction is not one of compassion for the other party but one of anger instead.

I can recite an incident from my past where I was not in a position to show compassion. But with time, God has worked in my heart to change the way I view the hurt. He also has used this pain to grow me up in Him where I can live beyond this incident.

The incident involved my father-in-law. He had said something that was hurtful. So I replied that he was not right, and asked him to apologize.

He refused my request, which led to our avoiding seeing each other for about one year -- although we lived fairly close to one another.

Eventually God worked on my heart and I asked for a meeting to reconcile our differences. I met one-on-one with him and told him I was sorry that this disagreement had led to a separation. I also said that I was ready to move beyond this incident, and I asked him if he would be willing to do that also.

He wanted the same thing and agreed to put this behind us. I believe God was at work in all of this because we have never had another disagreement, and our friendship blossomed. My father has passed away since this incident, and I am glad I have this deep friendship with my father-in-law, which helps lessen the loss I felt when my Dad passed.

I believe in part because I moved beyond this incident and God grew me up that I now have more compassion and don't immediately react with anger when offended. Also, when we fix our minds on Jesus, He blesses us.

> "When a man's ways are pleasing to the Lord, he makes
> even his enemies live at peace with him." Proverbs 16:7.

Now when offended I subconsciously think of the other person and realize that we all hurt and that none of us are perfect. I realize there will be hurt in life -that we are all broken and we all need healing- and therefore, instead of retaliating with one hurt for another, I can be compassionate and pray for them that God might provide healing for them as He did for me.

63. Just Do It - Quickly and Precisely

I sn't it encouraging to see some of the stalwarts in the Bible leading by example? I find it motivating, particularly reading of those who were instructed by the Lord to do a certain thing and then reading of the success they had in carrying it out.

Certainly there are stories in the Bible about people who did not follow the instruction of God. But I want to emphasize again that following the words of instruction precisely typically results in a great outcome. We see that sometimes the instructions are not pleasant, but still they must be carried out.

This was the case with Abraham. When God made a covenant with him to make him the "father of many nations." The Lord said Abraham's part of the covenant was to circumcise each male in his household, including those bought with money. This was a symbol of an everlasting covenant.

> "On that very day Abraham took his son Ishmael and all those born in his household or bought with his money, every male in his household, and circumcised them, as God told him." (Genesis 17:23)

So being a male I don't think that Abraham was exactly delighted to hear what was required of him and the other males, but he did not delay, He did it quickly, and God did bless him and he did become the father of many nations.

We see later in the Book of Numbers the repercussions of not precisely following the instructions from God. This is from when the Israelite community was in the desert. There was no water and so the community gathered in opposition to Moses and Aaron. Moses and Aaron took the problem to God and He said:

"'Take the staff, and you and your brother Aaron gather the assembly together. Speak to that rock [in front of the Tent of Meetings] before their eyes and it will pour out its water. You will bring water out of the rock for the community so they and their livestock can drink.'

"So Moses took the staff from the Lord's presence, just as he commanded him. He and Aaron gathered the assembly together in front of the rock and Moses said to them, 'Listen, you rebels, must we bring you water out of this rock?' Then Moses raised his arm and struck the rock twice with his staff. Water gushed out, and the community and their livestock drank.

"But the Lord said to Moses and Aaron, 'Because you did not trust in me enough to honor me as holy in the sight of the Israelites, you will not bring this community into the land I give them.'" (Numbers 20:8-12)

Wow! You mean the man that God chose to lead the Israeli nation out of Egypt — the guy that was placed in a papyrus basket in the river Nile, who was raised in the Pharaoh's household, who led them through the Red Sea, the guy who led the Israelites during the grumbling period in the wilderness — was not going to lead them into the Promised Land?

All because, instead of speaking to the rock, he struck the rock with his staff, as he had struck other items, like the River Nile and it turned blood red? I mean, that seems kind of harsh. But there is something else at play here. See, not only did Moses disobey God, but he also tried to take credit for what God had done!

Foot notes in *Life Application Bible* explain it this way: "The Lord had told him to speak to the rock; however, Moses struck it, not once, but twice. God did the miracle; yet Moses was taking credit for it when he said, "We bring you water out of this rock." It goes on to state, "Moses disobeyed God's direct command and dishonored God in the presence of his people." It is very important to follow God's commands and follow them precisely.

A final scripture I would like to cite is in Genesis 19 where the two angels are leading Lot and his wife and two daughters out of Sodom and Gomorrah before their destruction. The angels said to Lot and his family, "Flee for your lives! Don't look back, and don't stop anywhere in the plain" (Genesis 19:17).

But then in Genesis 19:26, we read: "But Lot's wife looked back, and she became a pillar of salt."

So we see here that the consequence of not following the direction of God's appointed angels was death. Although Lot's wife was in the journey, this act of disobedience cost her life.

So, as a follow-up to the gold nugget, Just Do It, not only should we do what we feel God is telling us to do, but to do it quickly and precisely according to God's leading.

64. Dreams

Dreams are important for all of us as they give us hope for the future, motivate us, and give us energy for life. Everyone likes to dream even from a young age. In the classrooms at elementary schools, teachers are always asking what you want to do when you grow up.

If you don't have a goal or don't have dreams for your future, you run the risk of becoming complacent while losing your motivation. Think about an elderly couple. How many times have you heard of where one of the two dies, and within two years, the spouse passes away? This is because without a living spouse there is little reason or goal for the living partner to continue on.

I was in attendance at Free Chapel Church, in Gainesville, Georgia on September 28, 2014 and enjoyed Jentezen Franklin's teaching on the subject of dreams. He used an acrostic poem for the word DREAM, in which:

D stands for Distinguish You,

R stands for Release your potential,

E stands for Encourage You,

A stands for Affect the Prevailing Attitude

M stands for Motivate You.

The Scripture reference was from when Joseph had his dream about his sheaf rising up and standing upright, while his brothers' sheaves gathered around it and bowed to it. (Genesis 37:7). Pastor Franklin said that dreams produce discipline because if you are going to attain them you must work hard at it and be patient.

This was certainly true for Joseph, who had to endure being thrown in a pit by his brothers and later being thrown in prison. This was certainly true for me in writing this book, also. For although I felt God leading me to write the book, and confirmation of that through several different occurrences, the pressures of operating a home inspection business distracted me during the summer. I became too busy and did not pick up my writing on it until February 2015, a year after my initial prompting!

I encourage you to think about what your dreams are. Ask God to show you what His will is for you if you. Or think about what you want to be doing 10, 20, or 50 years from now. Ask Him to make that happen. And do as Jentezen Franklin suggests: "Never allow circumstances to change the dream that God put on your heart."

65. Our Bodies: The Temples of God

We know from Genesis that we are created in the image of God. We also know from Genesis that God knew us when we were in the womb. God loved us and formed us in His image and He never stops loving us—no matter what we do. But we should not damage our bodies. We are living temples created for God to glorify Him and we should not take part in actions that do not bring glory to Him.

We get all the information we need to know about our bodies and our relationship to the Holy Trinity in 1st Corinthians 6:14-20. "By his power God raised the Lord from the dead, and he will raise us also. Do you not know that your bodies are members of Christ himself? Shall I then take the members of Christ and unite them with a prostitute? Never! Do you not know that he who unites himself with a prostitute is one with her in body? For it is said, 'The two will become one flesh.' But he who unites himself with the Lord is one with him in spirit. Flee from sexual immorality. All other sins a man commits are outside his body, but he who sins sexually sins against his own body. Do you not know that your body is a temple of the Holy Spirit, who is in you, whom you have received from God? You are not your own; you were bought at a price. Therefore honor God with your body."

Those are some heavy words when you think about them and digest them. While in our world of self-absorption—with selfies and other things which bring glory to ourselves—we think we are our own. Like the self-made millionaire or the sports superstar. But we are not our own; we are God's. He made us, He blesses us and He gives us free will to do what we want. But what we want should bring glory to God for He owns us, and we should honor God by honoring God with our bodies.

There are many ways to honor God with our bodies. First, we need to put the right stuff into our bodies. So it is important that we nourish our bodies from all of the foods that God created for us (and the animals). We should not put too much or too little into our bodies so that we become obese or unhealthily frail.

While drinking is not a sin, drinking to the point of drunkenness is a sin, and drunkenness can lead to alcoholism and diseases of the liver. If we are trying to glorify God we should not unduly put foreign drugs, especially strong prescription drugs, into our bodies—unless directed by a physician.

As this passage discusses most significantly, God wants to protect us from the destruction that sexual sin causes, so He made one of the commandments against adultery. In the *Life Application Bible*, there is a good explanation for this that reads, "God created sex to be a beautiful and essential ingredient of marriage (between a man and woman), but sexual sin—sex outside the marriage relationship—always hurts someone. It hurts God because it shows that we prefer following our own desires instead of the leading of the Holy Spirit. It hurts others because it violates the commitment so necessary to a relationship.

It often brings disease to our bodies. And it deeply affects our personalities, which respond in anguish when we harm ourselves physically and spiritually." Sexual relations, whether before marriage or while married with someone other than your spouse, have consequences. That is why God— as our loving Father—set up commandments to forbid sex outside of marriage.

66. Do You Have Rich Habits?

We have all heard that if you want to reach a goal you must have a game plan on how you are going to get there. This is the concept behind the book called *Rich Habits —The Daily Success Habits of Wealthy Individuals* by Tom Corley. Mr. Corley states that 85 to 88 percent of American millionaires are self-made, first-generation rich. His book discusses the secrets of the wealthy that you can learn to attain greater wealth in your life.

The following paragraph was taken from his website:

> For five years, Mr. Corley observed and documented the daily activities of 233 wealthy people and 128 people living in poverty, he discovered there is an immense difference between the habits of the wealthy and the poor. During his research he identified over 200 daily activities that separated the "haves" from the "have-nots."[5]

I have included a few of the more significant success habits in this book as I believe they set the stage and reveal much about why some people are successful and others are not.

One of Mr. Corley's findings is that seventy-six percent of wealthy exercise aerobically four days a week. Twenty-three percent of the poor do this. Obviously exercising is beneficial to our bodies and since our bodies are God's temple, He desires that we maintain a healthy body regardless of whether we are rich or not.

Another of Mr. Corley's findings is that "Sixty-seven percent of wealthy write down their goals versus 17% of poor." Most every leadership guru will tell you to write down your goals and monitor your progress towards

---

5. Tom Corley, www.richhabitsinstitute.com. The culmination of his research can be found in his number one best-selling book, *Rich Habits — The Daily Success Habits of Wealthy Individuals*.

them so this is obviously a key undertaking to put in place in your life regardless of what age you are.

I include mention of these habits and the book not because I believe you should be obsessed with attaining wealth. I understand that we are told in the Word that not money, but rather the love of money is the root of all kinds of evil (1 Timothy 6:10). I include mention of the book and cite a few habits because I think the book gives clear examples to the fact that there are habits that can be undertaken by all individuals that will better their lives. I believe Mr. Corley's book provides another tool which can be utilized by Christians and non-Christians alike to create a better life for themselves.

67. Positive Attitude

I believe that in the last six months God has been showing me how important it is to maintain a positive attitude. He has been showing me that not only must I keep a positive attitude to obtain the full life He has for me, but I must speak and think positive comments and thoughts. When we think or say, "I can't" that opens the door for the enemy negatively to impact us in various areas of our lives.

In 2 Corinthians 10:5, Paul admonishes us to think as Jesus would think: "We demolish arguments and every pretension that sets itself up against the knowledge of God, and we take captive every thought to make it obedient to Christ."

In the *Life Application Study Bible,* the application note for this verse is: "Paul uses military terminology to describe this warfare against sin and Satan. God must be the commander in chief—even our thoughts must be submitted to his control as we live for Him."

So, just as we cannot have two drivers in a car, we cannot think godly and speak worldly. God wants us to be filled with hope and joy, but if in our speech we are saying we can't do this or we can't do that, we are handicapping God. We must have an attitude as written in Philippians 4:13: "I can do everything through him who gives me strength."

When we begin thinking or spouting forth statements that are contrary to God's Word, we aid the enemy with his assault against our minds. If we have an attitude that "I can do this because of Christ who lives in me" and "I can do that because of His strength—mentally and physically," and speak these things, then God can use that and multiply that through His power to help us achieve or accomplish that which we are thinking or speaking.

68. Always Let Others Help You

This nugget is one that I have been pouring into the lives of my three daughters for many years. Many times our pride stands in the way of a greater relationship with others who are trying to help us. Even the disciples let this play out during the last supper in the Upper Room as Jesus began to wash their feet. What an excellent example of servant leadership our Savior gave us! Even though the disciples witnessed Him performing miracles and knew that He was the Christ, they allowed the King of Kings to wash their feet that night.

What if they had let their pride stand in the way? What if they had said, "No, you don't have to do that, I can do that"? Or, "please don't do that. It makes me feel uncomfortable"? Peter came very close to doing this but Jesus stopped him. This humble act was necessary for the Lord to teach His band of disciples the importance of humility and serving others.

God's will was done, and they opened up and yielded to the desires of their Lord, who wanted to show them that to be great you must be like the least. I believe it is significant that this is one of the last things Jesus did before His arrest. Thereby demonstrating to His disciples how to serve others.

Also, recall that Jesus had been on the receiving side of allowing others to serve Him, Mary poured the expensive perfume on Jesus' feet, drying them with her hair. In this story, told in John 12, the Savior not only allows Mary to use the expensive perfume on His feet, but corrects Judas when Judas objected to the use of this expensive perfume in such a manner.

If we would say yes, instead of letting our pride get in the way when we say no, the person offering help would feel better and we would feel a stronger, warmer tie with this person. An example would be if we are carrying a box and approaching the door in a public setting, and someone behind us offers to open the door.

We need to allow that person to help us and simply say, "Thank you." But many people (myself included, until God worked on my heart) would be tempted to say, "No, I can get it."

Or maybe you are at a friend's house during the summer when it is hot and they offer you something to drink. It might make them feel better, make them feel appreciated, if you say, "Yes." This is especially helpful if someone is aware of a monetary crisis you may be having, and they offer you cash or financial assistance to help you get through the difficulty. Don't allow pride, to be your first response. Many people say, "No, I couldn't accept this," and in doing so, miss God's blessing.

But let me explain how this worked in my family on two separate occasions. The first occasion occurred about eight years ago when a friend of my wife offered financial assistance to us around Christmas time. We were taken aback at first, because we didn't view our situation as needing outside help.

But my wife's friend had obviously picked up on some of her comments about the stress that our financial situation had created in our family. So, after we prayed on this and felt God leading us to accept the offer, my wife went back to her friend and said yes. As a result of her offer, and our acceptance, it provided further depth to the friendship, and we invited this friend to our house for dinner, where we got to know her even better.

A couple of years later, we were on the giving side of a situation, when friends of ours were going through a period of unemployment and needed some financial assistance. We learned of this need through a mutual friend, and so we purchased a Kroger gift card and gave it to them. The burden of groceries for the next week was removed.

We experienced on the giving end the joy that came from being in a financial position to be able to assist this family. I believe it opened our hearts to be more giving as we have contributed to the needs of others many more times after this first time.

69. Random Acts of Kindness

About 20 years ago, I worked for a company that was a service-based company. The president emphasized to all the service personnel how a small gesture could make a tremendous difference in a customer's satisfaction.

He also encouraged the service personnel to do small things, like learn the administrative assistant's birthday and give her or him a small gift on their birthday. This concept of doing something extra, of a small act of kindness stayed with me, and I used it when I started my home inspection. That concept is effective not only in business but in our personal lives also. If we each take time to reflect on how small random acts of kindness have impacted us, we are more likely to return the favor to others around us.

I'm sure you have had someone do something for you, that didn't cost anything or was just a small gesture, but it struck you and stopped you in your tracks because you were not expecting it. This recently happened to me.

I had begun attending group exercise classes at a local gym. At the end of a recent session, I was picking up my step platform and my weights and put them away. I came back to get my yoga mat, which the gym provides to put it away also.

As I picked it up, a lady in the class said, "I will take yours back with mine and put it away." I am sure I had a look in my eyes like a deer in headlights, as my brain was thinking, "You are also carrying your weights in your other hand, so I have less items to carry than you. As a man, I should be helping you by offering to carry your stuff." But then I thought about my belief to always accept help when someone offers it. So, that is what I did. I said, "Thank you," But this lady, who had never even spoken to me before, made a positive impact on my life because she caught me off guard and was there to help me.

I saw her regularly at the classes; and a couple of weeks later, I made a point to introduce myself and ask her name. I let her know that just a small random act of kindness like hers made me stop and take notice, and how it gave me a good feeling leaving the gym that day.

I thought to myself, "That is what we all should do: think of others and put a smile on their face by helping them in small ways when they are not expecting it." It doesn't cost anything, and isn't hard to do, but exercising these small gestures of kindness can sure make our lives a little more pleasant.

70. How to Achieve Your Goals

The ability to move forward and be successful in life is often linked to the capacity to formulate goals, and then to achieve or surpass those goals. Most successful people write down their goals, and they also write down a daily "To Do" list that is generally numbered according to priority. But getting back to setting and achieving goals, these are the larger items, the big picture ideas and milestones that you want to achieve.

These are goals you have contemplated for some time, discerning what it is you want to achieve. For the goal setting to be worthwhile, the goal must be specific and achievable. Setting a goal that you cannot achieve is self-defeating. So take time to formulate a goal that is reasonable, specific, and achievable.

Let's say you read the gold nugget, Financial Independence for Your Kids, and you decide that you want to jump start their financial independence by saving $1000 per year to place in their retirement account.

The best way to achieve this goal (or any goal) is to break it down into smaller tasks or steps. For example, if you want to have $1000 at the end of the year you could divide $1000 by 365 days. In that scenario, you know you need to save $2.74 per day.

You could also achieve that goal by eliminating money that you are spending elsewhere. Perhaps you decide to cut out a full priced lunch every day and substitute it with a value meal. That might save $2.74 per day. Or if you want to figure the amount of money to put away or save every week, you would divide the $1000 by 52 which results in saving $19.23 per week. On a monthly basis, this same computation yields $83.33 that would need to be saved per month.

The overriding principle here is that any goal can be broken down into smaller pieces, and that by measuring your performance in smaller intervals of time you have a greater likelihood of achieving your goal.

Let's say you make a New Years' resolution to lose 36 pounds by the end of the next year. The strategy is not to wait until the end of the year and see how well you measure up against the goal. To achieve your goal, the best strategy is to break this goal down into smaller chunks and measure your performance in smaller intervals.

My example of losing 36 pounds in 12 months can easily be divided to yield a monthly weight loss of 3 pounds per month. You could weigh yourself every month or even weekly to measure your progress towards the goal. This strategy will assist you in focusing on the goal more frequently—even on a daily basis—and it affords the opportunity to adjust the goals incrementally in either direction. It will also yield positive reinforcement if you are on pace for your goal.

Gold Nuggets Concerning God's Promises

71. Do Not Let Your Hearts Be Troubled

"Peace I leave with you; my peace I give you. I do not give to you as the world gives. Do not let your hearts be troubled and do not be afraid." John 14:27

Times have become very discouraging for a variety of factors. There is good reason for Christians, as well as all others to be troubled. Terrorists are active throughout Europe, the Middle East, Asia and Africa.

Daily news reports the activity of these terror cells, and Christians and non-Christians alike are killed each day. The federal deficit increases at an alarming rate and China, holds the largest percentage of the federal debt held by foreign countries.

Congress and the President are at odds, not to mention the United States being at odds with Iran, North Korea and Russia. The average take-home pay is stagnant or has been decreasing for several years in the United States, so families are struggling more now than a decade ago.

The Bible also reminds us there will be earthquakes and other natural disasters in the last days. In 2 Timothy 3:1 we read, "But mark this: There will be terrible times in the last days." It goes on in that chapter to describe situations present in today's society that are ungodly, and so we can see and feel and sense that we are in the last days. But should we despair and let our hearts be troubled? The answer is, "Definitely no." As Christians we should be the ones least troubled by the current state of world affairs.

Jesus died for us that we might have Him living in us, giving us faith and hope and love. In John 16:33 Jesus said, "In this world you will have trouble. But take heart! I have overcome the world." So regardless of what is happening in the world, regardless of what we are facing, we who have Jesus living within us, have overcome—we are overcomers.

Yes we can and should have peace in this world because as Christians we have Jesus! He is all we need, even in these terrible times. We need to stop allowing ourselves to be fearful and intimidated and cowardly and unsettled.

We need to put into practice the words of the apostle Paul from Philippians 4:6,

> "Do not be anxious about anything, but in everything, by prayer and petition, with thanksgiving, present your requests to God. And the peace of God, which transcends all understanding, will guard your hearts and your minds in Christ Jesus. Finally, brothers, whatever is true, whatever is noble, whatever is right, whatever is pure, whatever is lovely, whatever is admirable—if anything is excellent or praiseworthy—think about such things. Whatever you have learned or received or heard from me, or seen in me—put it into practice. And the God of peace will be with you."

So, do not let your hearts be troubled. Keep your eyes focused on Jesus. Follow His lead and think of the things He did and talked about. He is our Savior and He will give us peace in a world that is filled with trouble.

72. Trust In the Lord

One morning in early May of 2017 during my devotion time, the Holy Spirit was very present. The Holy Spirit revealed some things to me so that I could step forward with newfound confidence and power. I was in a great mood and was ready to move in that power and revelation for God's glory. I had an afternoon inspection scheduled and my client was going to come near the end of it and the seller was going to be home to let me in.

As I rang the doorbell for the inspection, the seller immediately opened the door. She had a great big smile on her face and I noticed she had a "Holy Land Experience" T-shirt on. She told me her name was Lisa, and I quickly responded that was my wife's name. She said that was so cool and I immediately felt a connection with her.

To confirm my intuition I asked her if she was a Christian and she gave a resounding "Yes." I told her I was too and she said "Oh, I tried to sell this house two years ago so I could move to California to be with my Dad, but it didn't work out. Now with you being a Christian, I believe this is a sign that it will work out this time."

As I began my inspection, she informed me that she had been to "The Holy Land Experience," and I told her I had been to the real Holy Land in Israel. We talked some more and discussed the churches we attend and then she informed me she speaks in tongues. I further learned through the various pictures of Angels and Scriptures that were framed in her house that she had deep religious convictions.

About halfway through the inspection, the client arrived and phoned me to let him in. When he did I answered him with the address "doctor" because that is how he referred to himself. He came in and while he was looking at the house Lisa, the seller, said to me "I need to talk to you." Because of my faith and our interaction up to this point in her house she felt comfortable confiding in me.

She said, "Daniel the realtor told me this buyer couldn't afford to pay closing costs so I agreed to pay them, but if he is a doctor I feel like he could afford to pay them and I have been mistreated."

I could see the dejection in her face and I knew she was happy to be selling this house because she had told me this when I first arrived. I assured her not to let what is going through your head cause her to worry. I went on to say, "About an hour ago you told me you were so happy to be selling this house. God has this and will work it all out."

A few minutes later God put this verse in my mind: Trust in the Lord with all your heart and lean not on your own understanding; in all your ways acknowledge him, and he will make your paths straight" (Proverbs 3:5, 6).

I went back to Lisa and recited that passage to her, but ended it with "He will make your path straight to California." She smiled and further confided in me that God had told her some time ago that He was going to move her to California and that He would find a good Christian man for her there that she would marry. I reaffirmed that we must trust God and when we do we will reap the blessings that come from trusting Him — blessings like getting to move to California.

What I explained to Lisa was that when God gives you knowledge like that, when He speaks to you and tells you something, grab hold of it and believe it with all of your might.

Satan may later try to make you doubt that or even say it is not going to happen but don't let him take away the promises of God. God has hammered that home to me on multiple occasions, and I have learned we do much better to listen to the promises of God than to listen what might be going through our heads.

This turned out to be the case for Lisa in the sale of her house. I believe that God showed her because of her doubt that this buyer would not buy this house, and the buyer backed out. I spoke to Lisa afterwards and told her to still believe God's words to her regarding selling her house and moving to California. She agreed with me that is what she would do and within a month she had another contract to sell her house for approximately $4000 more than the original contract. She was able to sell her house for the higher price and move to California when she believed with all her heart and trusted God's earlier promise to her.

This precept to trust God is confirmed in His word in 2nd Corinthians 1:20 which reads: "For no matter how many promises God has made, they are 'Yes' in Christ. And so through him the 'Amen' is spoken by us to the glory of God." Thank you Lord that when we trust in you the outcome is so much better than when we trust in our own ways.

73. Do Not Be Anxious

"Do not be anxious about anything, but in everything, by prayer and petition, with thanksgiving, present your requests to God. And the peace of God, which transcends all understanding, will guard your hearts and your minds in Christ Jesus. Finally, brothers, whatever is true, whatever is noble, whatever is right, whatever is pure, whatever is lovely, whatever is admirable—if anything is excellent or praiseworthy—think about such things."
Philippians 4:6-8

In this passage from Philippians, it is clear that God does not want us to be anxious. But do not be anxious about anything? That is a tall task — but one we should seek to attain.

Think about how little stress there would be if we did not get anxious over things. Think of how it would free us up in our relationships if we were honest with one another. But our anxiety keeps us from being open and truthful. We wonder what others think, but what would the other person think if we never put up a front? What if we had no anxiety in our dating life, or in our finances, or in dealing with family?

I believe Paul is leading us in verse 8 that in addition to the prayers and petition mentioned in verse 6 a key way to work towards eliminating anxiety in our lives is to focus on Godly things. God works in the supernatural and in some instances he may remove the anxiety when we pray instantaneously and other times He knows it will serve us better to let this transpire over time. But He hears our prayers and wants us to be free from all that hinders us, and certainly anxiety is one of those things. If in addition to prayers and petitions we begin to think about positive things, such as the grace of God, of His steadfast love for us, and of His Holiness, that will leave less time to focus on the stressful things, and will lead us down the path towards casting off our anxieties.

74. Tell God What You Want

We know that almost everyone prays. Even some agnostics have cried out to someone or something in a time of great need.

I believe that when we pray, we should focus our prayers on the needs of others and what God would want to occur in the world around us. It is also appropriate to pray for what we sense God leading us to seek and often this includes our needs and personal desires.

My experience has been that we often repeat the prayers that are really important to us. Many times, we bring them up as if God didn't hear us the first time. But He does. There are times that we may choose to keep a matter before the Lord in prayer not out of fear but out of faith as we believe that He will provide for us in amazing ways.

God knows the number of hairs on our heads and He hears our requests the first time, we pray. Actually, He knows the words of our heart even before we pray but prayer is an exercise of faith. When we pray, we proclaim that Jesus is Lord and He has the ability to work on our behalf.

Set a goal never to become impatience when you don't receiving immediate result. God's timing is not our timing and He may allow a problem or a need to continue for a season until we are ready to hear His plan or accept His course of action. Other times, He may just want us to wait in prayer believing that He has our best in mind and when the time is right, the door will open, the light will pour in, and your heart will be lifted.

Never allow your heart to grow discouraged. We are praying to God, the Creator of the universe—the Lord of all lords and the King of all kings. Is it our lack of belief that God will do something when we ask (the first time), that creates this desire to lift up the prayer request over and over?

Let's look at Matthew 7:11 to gain insight which is helpful in exploring this dilemma. This verse reads, "If you, then, though you are evil, know how to give good gifts to your children, how much more will your Father in heaven give good gifts to those who ask him!"

These are Jesus' words that follow the widely recognized, "ask, seek, and ye shall find" scripture teaching which Jesus spoke in verse 7. It reads "Ask and it will be given to you; seek and you will find; knock and the door will be opened to you." The verb tense in this verse is active, which means we are not to be faithless in prayer but we continue to hold up our request to Him. The persistent widow gained an answer to her request of Jesus. He even made note of it.

Here Jesus instructs us to ask for what we want but this is not an open invitation to ask for things outside of God's will. It is an instruction that when we ask in alignment with His will, we can expect an answer to be given.

If we believe when we first lift up our prayer request that it will be given to us, then we should acknowledge our belief when we repeat the request in subsequent prayers. We should not ask, and ask, and ask again. Rather we ask and immediately thank Him for granting our request. This is simply done by saying "Thank you, Lord, that You heard my prayer on XYZ, and because You love me greater than my earthly father, and because my will is in alignment with Your will, I believe that You are granting and fulfilling my prayer.

"I praise You, Lord, for answering this prayer, and I know that You work in spiritual realms with angels and archangels at Your side who are prepared to carry out Your every command. I thank You that You are a mighty God that hears my prayers and gives good gifts to those who ask."

A second Scripture that supports this concept—that we should pray and believe instead of praying the same prayer over and over—is Matthew 6:7. This verse reads, "When you pray, don't babble on and on as the Gentiles do. They think their prayers are answered merely by repeating their words again and again" (New Living Translation).

I believe God does not want us to pray the same prayer over and over, as if we have not said the prayer before or as if He did not hear us. Rather I believe He wants us to ask Him once, believe in our hearts He heard us and thank Him subsequently.

God does not answer every prayer immediately, but in His own perfect timing. Therefore, we should have faith and thank Him and say we know it will be answered. The biblical basis for this thought is Hebrews 11:1 which reads, "Now faith is being sure of what we hope for and certain of what we do not see."

Therefore, even if we don't see our prayer request answered on the day we pray it, we should believe that God has already heard it and will put into motion the supernatural, actions in the spiritual realms to bring about His will. There are differing opinions on Matthew 6:7, and some interpretations of this verse state that the repetition of words in some sort of magical incantation does not lend more credence to what you are praying.

I would concur with those opinions as from what I read in the Bible, Jesus spoke against many of the Pharisees' and rabbis' practices along these lines and appears to take more of a direct approach with comments such as, "Simply let your 'Yes' be 'Yes' and your 'No,' 'No.'" (See Matthew 5:37).

The Life Application Bible by Zondervan has an application note on Matthew 6:7 that states, "It's not wrong to come to God many times with the same requests—Jesus encourages persistent prayer."

I agree that if it is on our heart, just like an earthly father, God our Father wants to hear from us on it. I feel that He would prefer to hear, "Thank You. I believe You are answering my prayer for You are good. Or, I can't see what You are doing but in faith I believe You will address my prayer request."

The application note continues to say, "We can never pray too much if our prayers are honest and sincere." And then continues by adding, "Before you start to pray, make sure you mean what you say." These are both excellent comments as Jesus taught us to "pray without ceasing" and stated in Mark 11:24 "Therefore I tell you, whatever you ask for in prayer, believe that you have received it, and it will be yours."

Beyond these thoughts on telling God what we want in daily prayers (a micro look), I believe God wants us to think about the big picture for our life (a macro look) and then after we have thought about it, from time to time come to Him with our big issues and tell Him what we want.

It is my perception that most of us don't do that for one reason or another. It may be that we are too busy to take the time for this, or there is too much chaos going on around us in our life, or one of a myriad of other reasons. But I believe that unless we have a life coach or some other mentor-type figure in our life, we have a tendency not to go deep and explore; we just go through the motions in life.

In a previous church, I had a friend who would go away with his wife once every three months, just to strategize and re-focus. He and his wife would focus on what was best for their family, their business and develop goals for the future. Some of us may do this on our own, but we do this from our own strength, instead of drawing on God's wisdom. If we do this drawing from our own strength, knowledge and experiences, we may be missing blessings from God that He would desire to place upon us—if we looked to Him for the wisdom and strength.

In my case I was blessed to have my pastor, Kevin Myers, create an opportunity during church to do this. The way he set this up made it much more effective for me, and I suspect for many others in the congregation. Pastor Kevin wanted us to think about what we would tell God we wanted, but rather than just tell us to think of it in our minds, he made a big event out of it.

Although the church seats about 2700, he had the ushers pass out strips of red rubber about an inch tall and 8 inches long. Then he told the congregation to think about it and write down one thing we each wanted. Because of the way he set this up with time devoted during the service to pass out the red strips and then additional time allowed to write down what we wanted, it became a very impactful exercise.

That was about 8 years ago, and I wrote down, "To speak in front of large groups about Christ." Now I was not a pastor, nor did I operate a ministry for achieving this, and yet that was my heart's desire. While I did not understand it at the time, I believe God heard my "want" (as well as everyone else's in the congregation), and He honored it that day. And now

I believe this book will be the means to achieve that goal, because I have written about Godly concepts, and I will speak to churches and groups about the book. Had Pastor Kevin not provided that opportunity, I may well have never pondered the thought of speaking about Christ to groups, and additionally would not have communicated that to God.

Please think about what you really want—about what God would desire for you. Think about what would be good and pleasing to God. Also think about how God, the Creator and King of heaven and earth loves you and wants to give you the desires of your heart, if you will just ask Him. Then, as *The Life Application Bible* footnote stated, "make sure you mean what you say" and take it to the Lord in prayer, knowing that He desires to give you what you ask for. It may serve you well to write it in this book after thinking about it, just as I wrote it down in the church that Sunday. If something is troubling you or if you really have a passion for something, don't be timid. Consider this your opportunity like the opportunity my Senior Pastor gave me and tell God what you want! Be bold! I can assure you God wants to hear from you and he wants to give you your heart's desire.

75. Trust Him, Trust Him, Trust Him

In the time of Jesus when something was to be emphasized, it was spoken three times. For example, this occurred after Jesus was arrested; Peter denied knowing Him three times. Then when Jesus forgave Peter He asked him three times "Do you love me?" and three times Peter replied "Yes." Trust is closely related to faith and is very important, thus I have written this gold nugget title three times.

When I am performing a home inspection as one of my professional responsibilities, many times this issue of trust will come up. Sometimes the seller will list in the seller's disclosure statement that there was a water leak, but it has been repaired. The buyers will want me to check that area closely to confirm whether they can trust the seller's disclosure statement.

Another area that seems to be particularly troubling to some buyers is when there are boxes stored in front of the electric panel, which is in the garage. The sellers typically begin packing up before I perform the inspection, and store those boxes in the garage. Simply because I point out that I could not take the cover off the electric panel and look inside, some buyers become uneasy.

I am careful to explain to them and show them why I could not inspect this area, but they assume the worst, that there is a problem in the electric panel. When this occurs I point out there are many items such as the area between sheetrock walls, and in some areas in attics, where a home inspector cannot inspect. I go on to further explain that the inside of pipes or the ductwork in the house are not typically inspected, but that there is some degree of trust that the sellers are being forthright in their seller's disclosure statement that is required of the buyers.

The trust in a home sale transaction between the buyer and seller is analogous to what we as Christians must do if we want to grow in our faith; we must trust God. It isn't always easy, but we know He doesn't want us to worry about issues that are beyond our control. There are few certainties in life -other than death and taxes- and it really all comes down to trust. When you fly on a jet you are trusting that you will arrive safely, and statistically speaking, there are less airline passenger deaths per mile flown than deaths per mile driven by car. We know that God is for us and wants the best for us. But we often tend to fall away from the Bible's teachings and get caught up in earthly thoughts instead of the promises of Heaven.

We would do well to trust in the words of Jeremiah 29:11 which reads,"'For I know the plans I have for you,' declares the Lord, 'plans to prosper you and not to harm you, plans to give you a hope and a future.'" There are many other promises in the Bible; we should trust and acknowledge that He is faithful and has a way and a plan for us that is no doubt better than any we have. Trusting Him and living out this trust will not only strengthen our faith but also be less stressful in the process. So let's trust Him, trust Him, trust Him!

Gold Nuggets for Financial Freedom

76. The Blessed Financial Path

We all want to see our children succeed. One of the areas you can help your children succeed is in financial matters. If you prepare yourself, by the time they are twenty you can set them on the path to financial freedom. The key is to understand the "time value of money," which refers to the fact that money earns interest and can work for you, or against you.

If used wisely "the time value of money" can reap tremendous dividends for the investor or in our case, for our children. The younger you get started on this concept the better, and the sooner you explain this to your children the better off they will be financially as well, if they implement the practice.

My cousin Barry Flagg, a Certified Financial Planner, taught me this when I was about thirty years old. He said a person would be better off if they began investing $1000 per year when they were twenty years old for ten years—and then stopped—than if they started investing $1000 per year at age thirty and continued for thirty-five years.

At age sixty-five the younger investor would have more money accumulated because of the "time value of money", the amount of money gained because of compounded interest, like a snowball growing in size as it rolls down a hill. For example, investing $1000 per year at an 8 percent return beginning at age twenty for ten years (a $10,000 total cash outlay) would yield $231,000 by age sixty-five.

By comparison, investing $1000 per year beginning at age thirty for thirty-five years (a $35,000 total cash outlay) would yield a substantially lower $186,000 by age sixty-five. Getting started early really makes a difference. Consider if your child started investing $1000 per year at age twenty and continued without stopping until the age of sixty-five, the $231,000 would be added to the $186,000 to total $417,000, not a bad nest egg.

This motivated my wife and me to set up and contribute to a Roth IRA for our oldest daughter when she turned twenty. We continued this for two years until she graduated from college and was employed so she could contribute to it herself.

We went over these numbers with her and explained how she could set herself on the road to financial independence by continuing the $1000 per year investment that we began for her. We also contributed $1000 for two consecutive years to our middle daughter after she turned 20 and plan to do the same with our youngest daughter when she turns twenty.

The great part about this nugget is that just like in training kids to do anything, you explain the situation to them, help them by making the first two $1000 investments (akin to pushing a bike for them to ride the first time), and then you let them take over and follow through.

Encourage them in years three and above to continue the investment, and they will have financial security that few have as they grow up. Furthermore you will have imparted to them financial wisdom as they begin to venture out on their own. As I was preparing this book I asked my oldest daughter if she set aside $1000 each year for the two years since college. I was heartened to have her answer that she had set it up as an automatic draft out of her payroll check. She had continued what my wife and I set up with no encouragement or prompting. That is a great financial start for her and a gratifying blessing to my wife and me.

77. Tithing

The word "tithe" literally means "one-tenth" and is found in many locations in the Old Testament. While the concept is not found in the New Testament, the principle still applies today. The idea of giving a tenth of one's income originated in the time of Moses [see Leviticus 27:30-34]. Then, in the last book of the Old Testament, Malachi, God speaks through Malachi to tell Israel they are robbing the Lord.

Verse 8 of Malachi 3 says, "'will a man rob God? Yet you rob me. But you ask, 'How do we rob you?'" And the Lord replies "in tithes and offerings." The passage goes on to challenge the nation of Israel to "bring the whole tithe into the storehouse, that there may be food in my house." Since the church is believed to be the place where believers get their spiritual "food", the idea is to give the tithe to the church you attend.

Often people have mixed feelings about tithing, but I think the important idea here is the state of your heart. Ideally, we freely give because we love the Lord. We give out of gratitude for what He has done for us in the past and what we know He will do in the future.

God's Word tells us that He loves a "cheerful giver" and so does the world. Giving is received by most all as kind, caring and compassionate. Giving away helps us to loosen our dependence on material things, which brings into focus more clearly the things of God.

My parents taught me when I was very young to give to the church, and, before I was married, I held a position in my local fellowship where I formally encouraged the congregation to give.

After I married, we experienced financial difficulties and I let our family's giving dip below ten percent. It was my dear wife, who pointed out that I was adjusting our giving according to our circumstances rather than being committed to tithing first and then trusting that God would provide for our needs.

I now regret making those knee-jerk reactions in our family's finances, but I am so grateful that my wife put me back on the right track to tithing.

Our family has been blessed innumerably since my wife pointed out my shortsightedness, and this is true of most everyone once they commit to a tithe, they are blessed beyond anything they had imagined.

78. Don't Borrow Against A Home's Equity

Clark Howard is a nationally-syndicated radio personality who has a large presence in Atlanta where he is based. He is a consumer guru, offering advice through his call-in radio show and through his website, and is a well-known speaker. He has offered some sound advice, which I observed and wanted to include as a gold nugget. He said *not* to borrow against a home's equity.

I think he was directing this towards those that have little or no equity in their house, or those that have a great deal of equity and decide to borrow a good portion of that equity. His reasoning was that if you borrow against a home's equity and lose your job this could cause you to lose your house. I agree with him that a house is your largest investment, and in general, you don't want to risk losing that by borrowing against it.

We find in the bible that the borrower is slave to the lender and so we should if at all possible keep from borrowing money. For a large purchase like a house almost everyone will need to borrow money, but we should keep borrowing to a minimum and pay off loans as quickly as possible. Thus if we take out home equity loans we are going in the opposite direction from what God would have us to do - we are increasing the amount we owe. Therefore we should attempt never to use a home's equity to purchase things which have a shorter life than a home. Preferably we should save money until we can pay cash for smaller items than a house.

79. Beyond A Tithe

In an earlier gold nugget I spoke about tithing, the practice of giving one tenth of your income back to the Lord through your local church. This is what God commands us to do, and when we obey His commands, he blesses us. What I want to discuss in this gold nugget, is going beyond a tithing, giving more than one tenth to the church.

Pastor Robert Morris presented his teaching on tithing at 12 Stone Church in 2014. In his book, *The Blessed Life*, Pastor Robert Morris discusses unlocking the rewards of generous living. One of the chapters is entitled the "Principle of Multiplication."

Mr. Morris made a compelling presentation that when you give above 10 percent it allows God to multiply the blessings that you receive for the generosity in your heart. The backdrop for this teaching is Luke 9, which is the account of Jesus feeding the five thousand with two fish and five loaves of bread.

In this chapter Mr. Morris states there are two principals at play in the principle of multiplication. First something must be blessed before it can multiply, in other words it has to be given to the Lord first.

Second it must be *given* rather than returned to the Lord. Pastor Morris believes that up to the 10 percent level we are simply returning to the Lord what is already his. It is only on the amount above 10 percent that the multiplication can occur on.

By multiplication he means receiving back more than you give. Mr. Morris has experienced this several times in his life. So our goal should be to be generous, to give above the 10 percent level so that God can leverage this additional giving for the good of the Kingdom. In so doing we will be blessed even greater than if we simply tithe.

Gold Nuggets
for Parenting

80. Change Up the Landscape

In parenting, when you really have something significant to convey to your children, change the environment to pack added punch to your communication.

One day, I wanted to speak to our daughters about a matter of great importance. At the time, they were only two, five, and eight-years old. But I wanted their undivided attention. So I asked them to sit side by side on the sofa in the family room.

Then I did something I had never done: I took one of our kitchen chairs, brought it to the family room and sat facing the girls. As young girls, this unique new seating arrangement captured their curiosity, and they could barely wait to see what I would say.

You would have thought I was going to tell them the sky was falling. I had their attention because the seating arrangement was completely out of the ordinary; they didn't know what was going to happen. The simple action of changing up the landscape focused their attention on my words.

Children love the unexpected, the spontaneous, and also the traditional. Anything that deviates from the day-to-day routine can capture their attention. Consider using a celebration plate, a different color from the rest of your dinner plates on significant days. Some plates can be inscribed with personal phrases such as "Special Person of the Day."

The plate is reserved for any special occasion - a birthday, or even the day one of your children brings home a report card with good grades. Set the plate on the table when a son has acted kindly to someone or when a daughter has made her first hit in peewee league. You get the message: look for ways to make them feel special.

The more frequently you find reasons to celebrate the better. You may find yourself going on a "treasure hunt" for the good they do and rewarding them for it, overlooking things, which formerly irritated you.

Your outlook may change as you think from a different perspective, appreciating aspects of your children that you see more clearly because you are focusing on positive elements in their lives.

81. Bring in a Mentor

"Train a child in the way he should go, and when he is old he will not turn from it. " Proverbs 22:6

Today, our youth often fall away from the path God would have for them and embrace many dark things of this fallen world. At younger and younger ages children get involved in drugs and sex and many other things like guns and violence, especially in the inner city. Yet as Christian parents, we need to ask ourselves if we are rearing our children according to this verse in Proverbs.

Training children in the way they should go can take time and with our busy lifestyles, many of us rarely have time to even eat meals together. Finding time for family devotions that include prayer and Bible reading is especially difficult. Yet the Bible encourages us to be diligent in teaching our children about our religious heritage and the salvation that is ours through Jesus Christ.

In Deuteronomy 11:18-19 God instructed the Israelites to "Fix these words of mine in your hearts and minds…" and to "Teach them to your children, talking about them when you sit at home and when you walk along the road, when you lie down and when you get up." (Note: This passage uses the story of the Exodus only as a springboard to urge the active remembering of God's words.)

We made extra effort in our family to have devotions daily. But many times we were sporadic and inconsistent. Yet in reading these scriptures from the Old Testament, we saw that God expected us to discuss scripture with our children throughout the day. Talking with our children as we completed our chores, prepared our meals, and drove on errands became an easy, stress-free way to communicate our faith.

As our children grew, however, we felt they would benefit from the influence of others outside our family who sincerely loved the Lord. A caring mentor who meets regularly with a child can greatly assist parents in the guiding and teaching spiritual principles, supporting and echoing foundational truths, and talking and listening as a trusted friend.

Our family was blessed to have a situation evolve, when Ashley, a young Christian youth leader at our church asked to mentor our youngest child, Megan. For two years, Ashley met our daughter Megan, who was 13, and another girl every week at a restaurant near our church. She mentored the girls in many aspects of Christian living, including the virtues of dressing modestly and reserving sexual intimacy for marriage. Her positive impact on Megan was tremendous.

Because of the positive changes we saw in Megan, we began a search for a mentor for our middle daughter who also was named Ashley, as she entered her senior year of high school. We felt it was imperative she have an opportunity to develop the close relationship with a woman outside the family—someone who would support our values but be a step away from the close relationship she shared with her mother.

We wanted her to know that we acknowledged she might feel more open to sharing certain confidences with a trusted mentor. That would be important — a mentor as a resource to guide and counsel her as to which college to attend and as a resource to call upon as she went away for college.

Like our first daughter to be mentored, our second daughter grew and developed during her year of mentoring. The mentorship helped her developed a deep bond with this mentor and she looked forward to meeting with her. As a direct result of this mentoring relationship when she left for college, our daughter had her feet firmly grounded in a Christian worldview.

My hope is by recounting the mentoring of two of my children you have been stimulated to think of someone who might serve as a mentor for your children. I know you want the best for your child. Mentoring is all about desiring more for your children and taking action by supplementing the Christian values you instill in your children with additional resources to further stimulate and develop your children.

Start with prayer and then invest some time and effort brainstorming about the person who might be that specific mentor in your child's life. Pray also for someone who will partner with you as a parent and God to pour in love and support during the impressionable years, helping to draw out new and beautiful aspects of your child's character for His glory.

82. Be a "Yes" Dad or Mom

Saying "Yes" to our children as often as possible is crucial. This doesn't mean we agree to foolish requests; rather, we make every effort to support our children's wise decisions when we can.

During our children's younger years, I was a home inspector and used my evenings after dinner to type my inspection reports. Often our daughter Ashley would ask me, "Will you come out and play basketball with me, Dad?" I had a choice: work on my reports or spend time with Ashley.

I would struggle inwardly. The reports were due the next day before I went out for inspections again. Yet I knew that fostering a close relationship with our daughter was also important. How was I to choose? Have you ever been there?

Finally, I realized if Ashley was asking me to play basketball, then that was important to her. And if that was important to her, then it was important for *me* to let her know I valued her by choosing to play basketball with her when she asked, I let her know she was more important to me than my work.

Of course, I could have told her, "Yes, I will come out when I finish my work." But putting her before my work showed her she was a priority in my life. So I made it a habit to say "Yes" whenever she asked me to play with her. Many times we would be playing in our driveway when other neighborhood kids would join us, their parents still in their houses. They all knew I would often be in the driveway playing basketball, softball, or kickball because I had made a routine of being with our kids.

I once heard a story where a widow was thinking about how she had always hated that her husband forgot to put down the toilet seat after he used the bathroom. She always complained to him about his annoying habit. But after he passed away she thought to herself, "Oh, if he could only be here now I would never complain again about the toilet seat not being put down."

This is much how I see our time with our kids: when we're older will we look back and think, "I wish I would've spent more time at the office? I think not. We only have a short time when our children are with us. And an even shorter period of time when they *want* to spend time with us.

Make a decision to say "Yes!" as often as possible when they approach you, desiring to share a small slice of your life. Remember the song, *Cats in the Cradle* by Harry Chapin? It wasn't long in the child's life before he was telling his father, "I don't have time for you, Dad."

The boy grew up just like his father who didn't have time for him earlier in his life. Make the most of your time with your kids and let them know they are important to you.

83. Volunteer in Your Child's Classroom

Going to school with your child to help in his classroom speaks volumes to him about your support. Start early—when he is in kindergarten, if possible—and model cheerful voluntary involvement. Teachers encourage parental help, of course, so that they might focus more on education rather than on administrative tasks and "crowd control." But they also know parents can more effectively understand academic efforts and social interactions if they witness the child's behavior firsthand.

And what a positive experience it is for a child to see that his mother or father wants to join him in his world away from home! When a parent shows an interest in his child's educational world, the child may feel more empowered and confident as his self-esteem grows.

Participation in classroom activities also can provide a springboard for later dialogue between parent and child, where compliments can be voiced around the dinner table about the child's positive behavior at school: "I sure liked the way you shared your pencils with the girl next to you today."

The child gets a sense of teacher and parent being on the same side to support and encourage, especially when discussion is invited by such questions as, "I like the way the teacher did this; did you like that too?"

Volunteering in your child's classroom also allows observation of unfavorable conduct you may want to address later. Teachers occasionally invite parents into the classroom for this specific purpose, knowing that parents may only see one side of their child's behavior at home. Generally children act the same in both places, but occasionally a child acts differently at school than he does at home. Volunteering in the classroom provides an opportunity for you to see if your child behaves consistently in both places.

Helping in the classroom can also shortcut problems that may develop academically, allowing you to catch problem areas as they arise. If a work schedule prevents volunteering on a regular basis taking a half-day or a couple hours to observe and assist every couple of months would also be valuable. The idea is to model a heart to serve, uplifting the child by your presence while gaining valuable information about his overall performance both academically and socially. Strive to make this happen early. My children like most children would have no part of my volunteering or visiting in middle school, but enjoyed it in elementary school.

84. Let Your Kids See You Helping Others

All of us like to help others but with our hectic lifestyles it is difficult to fit it into our schedules. Many of us do help through group activities such as being an athletic coach or volunteering in the church nursery.

Obviously this fills a big need if we are going to have healthy communities with parents assisting with community activities. Most of these activities are organized and structured and become part of our regular routine. However, they essentially become part of the work that we must get done each week as parents.

I believe a beneficial experience for your children is to let them observe you stepping out of your routine to help others in need. This would be considered a random act of kindness rather than something you already committed to and must do.

These random acts of kindness set an example that will hopefully impact your kids and set the stage for them to undertake a random act of kindness themselves. Some random acts of kindness can simply be an act of courtesy such as opening a door for someone behind you or perhaps assisting the elderly with climbing up a set of stairs.

I think the random act of kindness will be remembered as more significant the more it takes us out of our routine. Hopefully it will be remembered longer and have a greater impact on our kids if it is inconvenient or more out of our way.

As an engineer, I have always been task oriented, making me less likely to veer from the task or goal I had in mind and help others. However, God began working on my heart after committing my life to Christ, and I began to think of others more than I had previously.

I think many are naturally gifted with this disposition, my wife included, but for me it has been a journey. As part of this journey there was one instance, which had a significant impact on my family.

My family and one of my daughter's friends were traveling in our van on an interstate to the lake on a Saturday morning. While driving south on the interstate I noticed a column of steam coming from the hood of a car parked on the shoulder of the northbound lanes.

It was obvious that this release of the steam had just started from the car's radiator. I decided to exit at the next exit and travel back to see if the driver needed additional water or anti-freeze. When we arrived the steam was no longer escaping. I asked him if we could help in any way but he said, "No", and explained that he had called a friend who was already on his way.

Even though I wasn't able to help this stranger, I did show my willingness to provide help and deviate from our immediate goal of getting to the lake. I am sure that many reading this book have the natural gift of helping and don't have to focus on helping ahead of time, as it will come naturally. For myself and others for whom this does not come naturally, contemplating actions you could take ahead of time and praying for God to put circumstances in your path where you can demonstrate random acts of kindness may provide an excellent teaching opportunity for your children.

85. Reconsider Your Child's College Options

When our middle daughter Ashley was in eighth grade, I attended a meeting at her school regarding college planning. The principal related information I had never heard before, a "gold nugget" that was to become profoundly significant in the life of our oldest daughter Kaitlyn who was sixteen at the time.

The principal referred to *Colleges That Change Lives: 40 Schools That Will Change the Way You Think about Colleges* by Loren Pope. The principal told us that Mr. Pope, the author of the book, had worked in education for over thirty years and had researched which colleges had the greatest positive impact on students.

His research revealed that small colleges (those with enrollment of less than two thousand) were the most gratifying for students. He suggested that the parents of bright high school students might reconsider the accepted strategy of sending their children to Ivy League or other top schools.

At these institutions, the class size may be well over two hundred students. The professor did not teach much of the time because he was doing research for grants. Instead, a teaching assistant actually provided the instruction.

Mr. Pope pointed out that, because of the large class size, no bond developed between the student and the professor unlike that which developed in smaller schools where the class size was only fifteen to twenty students. In the smaller schools, relationships were more personal. Professors would notice a student's absence in class, and many would travel overseas to accompany their students on summer studies.

Now, as I said before, the mention of this book came at a perfect time for our oldest daughter Kaitlyn. As a junior in high school, she had earned a high grade point average and could have probably gone to most any college, but she intentionally restricted her search to colleges in the southeastern United States because she wanted to attend a college reasonably close to our home in the greater Atlanta area. So while she did travel to and consider larger schools like North Carolina, Duke, and Georgia, she began to understand some of the differences between larger and smaller schools.

Eventually she narrowed her search and attended Birmingham Southern College—one of the smallest schools she considered—primarily because of its high academic standards and the fact that it offered a degree in dance. Kaitlyn desired to earn a dual major in math and dance, and most other schools offered only minor degrees in dance.

Her experience at Birmingham Southern was most gratifying and she found most of the premises of the book to be true. Class sizes were small and she developed strong ties with the professors. Even the President of the college kept the phone numbers of many students on his cell phone, including our daughter's! This demonstrated just how committed these educational professionals were to the success of their students.

Of course, different colleges are meant for different people, and by no means would I recommend eliminating larger colleges in the college search strictly based on the concepts in Loren Pope's book. I attended Georgia Tech, a school with a great reputation in my field. When I graduated I had the choice of many employment offers, although my GPA was low, because of the great reputation Georgia Tech enjoys in business and academic circles.

Praying well in advance of your child's college years, asking God to direct the decision, will prepare your hearts for the search. We were convinced during those later high school years that God was leading us and following His direction resulted in the best possible outcome for Kaitlyn.

This positive experience paved the way for Ashley, our second daughter, to consider smaller colleges when she began her research. Eventually she too was led to attend a small college.

Our third child, Megan took a different route, enrolling at a slightly larger school with enrollment of about 6000, because it was rated #1 in the country in her desired field of study. Therefore, I believe restricting your search for colleges to those under 2000 students in size might be overly restrictive, but that one should be aware that there are many advantages students enjoy at smaller schools that should be weighed when making a college decision.

86. Duties of a Father

In our journey of learning to be good parents in raising our family, we have all probably run across different sources of information and advice -- through friends, articles or materials on the Internet, or through resources at church.

This is the case for me and my wife, who have used and gleaned tidbits from various sources of information that have helped us to guide and direct our children's lives. Certainly, it didn't all come from within our minds.

This is certainly the concept behind this book. While many of these nuggets are our original thoughts, some are things we've learned along the way. I wanted to share some of the ones we have most benefited from.

One source that my wife and I ran across when our children were young is a program called "Growing Kids God's Way." It is a program developed by Gary and Anne Marie Ezzo, through their organization Growing Families International, Inc. In the program workbook we received, I made note of the eight duties of a father, and I felt they were worthy of restating below.

Cultivate a sense of family identity.

Demonstrate love to your wife.

Respect your children's private world.

Give children freedom to fail.

Be the encourager of the family.

Guard your tongue and tone and measure responses against the excitement on your kids' faces.

Connect with your children through physical touch.

Build trust based on God's Word and not on man's wisdom.

I think this is a good list. Certainly there are other items that you will need to do in being a good Dad, but if you just do these eight, you will be far ahead of most fathers.

87. Hire a Tutor

Recently my wife and my oldest daughter, who was formerly a math teacher, began tutoring a friend's daughter. After two weekly tutoring sessions, my wife was speaking to the friend and telling her that she wouldn't be able to tutor her daughter during the third week because of a busy schedule.

When the friend relayed this to her daughter, her daughter said "Oh, I like going over to the Flagg's house for tutoring." So she was disappointed that she was going to miss an opportunity for tutoring at our house.

I include this gold nugget for a couple of reasons. First, most kids like one-on-one attention. In this respect, tutoring is akin to the gold nugget on mentoring. I think it is very positive to have an adult or older teenager spend time to impart some of their knowledge or wisdom to a child.

Most children appreciate having someone more knowledgeable assist them with a subject they are struggling with. Additionally, I think that tutoring is such a positive influence that, even if the student has a "B" in the subject, spending time with a tutor is uplifting and motivating, and that most children would be like our friend's child and look forward to it.

In today's society, it's important to have your children look forward to a positive thing, like tutoring on a weekly basis. I think it is important to establish any activity in your child's life that they anticipate with enthusiasm. And then there is the obvious, that tutoring can result in substantially higher grades for the student, which in turn will make the student feel better about themselves.

My daughter, Kaitlyn, often tutors three or four students each week. While I don't keep close tabs on each one's performance, I do know that she tells me many of them were failing in math before enlisting her services as a tutor. And I know that most of them will pull their grades up as she tutors them. This seems to be the general trend across the spectrum of students that are tutored, regardless of whether they are male or female or whether they are taking algebra or another subject.

So if you are going to hire a tutor, how do you decide who to hire? A referral from a friend who has used the tutor would be one of the best sources of information. Or ask your student's teacher for a referral to a good tutor would be another source.

Gold Nuggets
to Overcome
Satan's Attacks

88. We Are the Security Keepers

We are the security keepers to our hearts. In the world there are many things which want to enter our hearts, corrupt our minds and mess with our souls. As Christians, it is important that we realize that we are not supposed to be like the rest of the world. We are supposed to stand in God's truth and not be swayed by the ways of this world.

We need to stand firm in His love when temptation comes along and not succumb to the things that bring those down who are far from God. This world wants to weigh us down. Offerings of alcohol, sex, and drugs are prevalent and the enemy wants to use them to wreck our lives. But we need to turn to Jesus and keep our eyes on Him.

The first step to standing firm is to realize that there is both good and bad in the world—and we have to protect our hearts, minds and souls. Yes, we must be the security keepers to our hearts; we must shield our hearts from all that wants to hurt us.

There are many things which seem innocent that in reality are things that will pull us slowly away from God and towards a darker life, a life that's void of God. While writing this book, I read that in the Miami regional headquarters of FIFA (the Federation Internationale de Football Association), seven of the top-level executives were arrested on racketeering charges.

Simultaneously in Switzerland, at the worldwide headquarters of FIFA, Swiss police arrested seven soccer officials at the request of U.S. prosecutors. Four other soccer and marketing officials who were affiliated with FIFA agreed to plead guilty.

Most of those arrested are accused of accepting bribes to place soccer games in certain countries. The insidious ways that the Enemy entices us takes many shapes and forms, but always takes us away from the truth of the Word of God. The men who accepted these bribes opened the gates of their heart as their lust for more money and greed got the best of them.

I wonder had they realized that once they let the corruption into their hearts the Enemy, the Devil, would tell them it is okay, and their moral compass would be forever changed. Once they said, "yes" initially, their minds told them, "Okay, we have accepted a bribe once, and so it won't be as significant an issue to say, 'yes' to corruption again." That is what these men are charged with—racketeering, which is a continued practice of corruption, with years of taking bribes.

It is critical that we realize we have to protect our hearts. There are decisions to allow good into our hearts, and there are decisions to keep the bad out by closing the gates to our hearts. We will be faced with both options. When it's time to make the decisions, we need to be prepared *before* the decision is made—to always guard our hearts, to never let the Enemy corrupt our hearts.

In Proverbs 4:23 it reads: "Above all else, guard your heart, for it is the wellspring of life." These are powerful words written by the person most Christians believe is the wisest man to ever live, Solomon.

The first three words, "Above all else" exclaim how important it is to guard our hearts, for everything comes from the heart. There is a song by Casting Crowns, entitled *Slow Fade*, which I have long used as an example of how when things change from black and white—from good and evil—to shades of gray, what a slippery slope it becomes. We need to always guard our hearts, always turn away from evil, because it becomes a slippery slope when we begin to condone something that is anything but good.

Here are a few of the verses of the song *Slow Fade* by Casting Crowns. I hope they will be helpful for you to become the "Security Keeper" of your heart.

Be careful little eyes what you see
It's the second glance that ties your hands as darkness pulls the strings
Be careful little feet where you go
For it's the little feet behind you that are sure to follow

It's a slow fade when you give yourself away
It's a slow fade when black and white have turned to gray

Thoughts invade, choices are made, a price will be paid
When you give yourself away
People never crumble in a day
It's a slow fade, it's a slow fade

89. Give the Enemy No Foothold

For our struggle is not against flesh and blood, but against
the rulers, against the authorities, against the powers of
this dark world and against the spiritual forces of evil in
the heavenly realms. Ephesians 6:12

Have you ever felt there is a battle going on around you? Have you ever felt there is a battle going on within you? Well, there is. Particularly if you are a Christian and doing strong works for the Lord. Honestly, the enemy has set you in his sights. He wants to take you down and render you ineffective for the Lord.

Are you married? The enemy wants to destroy your marriage. Do you have children? The enemy wants to turn them against you and cause them to turn away from God. Anything that God set up – marriage, the blessing of children, and the church – the enemy wants to tear down. This is because He is the archenemy of God and you belong to the Lord.

When my wife and I were going through a rough time in our marriage, she went on a weeklong vacation with our kids while I stayed at home to work. I called her while she was on vacation and spoke a sincere apology to her that I felt God had put on my heart. I asked her to forgive me for what I had said or done in the past.

When she arrived back from the vacation we had a very open discussion and reconciled our differences. During this conversation she told me, and I agreed, that at times it felt like Satan was between us, trying to pull us apart.

I'm aware that this didn't stop with her acceptance of my apology and our reconciliation. This is an ongoing battle in which the enemy works to take down our marriage, because God instituted marriage and anything God is for, the enemy is against.

So how do we fight against the enemy that is trying to destroy anything that stands for God, including us? The first thing is to acknowledge that there is an enemy and that he is not for us; he is against us.

We must recognize that the enemy is a fallen angel that wanted to be greater than God, so he was thrown out of heaven and took many angels from heaven with him which set up the ongoing conflict between good and evil that is referred to above in this passage from Ephesians. From Revelation 12:7-9 it reads: "And there was war in heaven. Michael and his angels fought against the dragon, and the dragon and his angels fought back. But he was not strong enough, and they lost their place in heaven. The great dragon was hurled down—that ancient serpent called the Devil, or Satan, who leads the whole world astray. He was hurled to the earth, and his angels with him."

Another thing we can do is to recognize that Satan is a defeated foe. Through Jesus Christ's death on the cross the victory is ours, and we will have eternal life if we acknowledge Jesus as our Lord and Savior.

If we acknowledge that Satan is very real indeed – that he is mentioned in the Old Testament, and Jesus spoke of him in the New Testament, and that we claim the promise in Christ that Satan is a defeated foe, is he going to leave us alone? The answer is a loud, "NO!"

So how do we win the battle, how do we remain upbeat each day although we are experiencing spiritual attacks daily? We must have a positive mindset that is set in the fact that Jesus loves us and is for us. We must read the Word, which is Jesus Christ, and proclaim passages like *Romans 8:31*, "If God is for us, who can be against us," and Philippians 4:13, "I can do everything through him who gives me strength."

It is a mindset; we must acknowledge it is a battle and just like soldiers on the battlefield we must engage the enemy. We must proclaim the good news of Jesus Christ who offers salvation and redemption to all who proclaim Jesus as their Lord and Savior. We must get in the Word. We must put on the full armor of God that is listed in Ephesians 6. Are you ready to put your armor on to save your soul and the soul of others around you?

I want to share with you two things that I have found invaluable in my battles. It will take more than this to win the battle, it will take the full armor of God and all the other resources we have as Christians. But these are two that have been key for me as I face my spiritual battles daily.

The first is a song I listen to and shout aloud the words as it is being played, usually first thing in the morning. The song is "Our God Reigns," by John Waller.

The second is a prayer I compiled from the book *Wild at Heart* by John Eldredge. The prayer is in John Eldridge's book but spread out over several chapters so I have compiled it into one prayer. Again this is a great weapon to use first thing in the morning against the battles you encounter that day.

Full Armor of God Prayer

Lord, I put on the belt of truth. I choose a lifestyle of honesty and integrity. Show me the truths I so desperately need today. Expose the lies I'm not even aware that I am believing.

And yes, Lord, I wear your righteousness today against all condemnation and corruption. Fit me with your holiness and purity – defend me from all assaults against my heart.

I do choose to live for the gospel at any moment. Show me where the larger story is unfolding and keep me from being so lax that I think the most important thing today is the soap operas of this world.

(Feet fitted with readiness from the gospel of peace section -- I love this part to seek the larger story rather than being consumed with the soap opera of the day)

Jesus, I lift against every lie and every assault the confidence that you are good, and that you have good in store for me. Nothing is coming today that can overcome me because you are with me. *(Shield of Faith section)*

Thank you, Lord, for my salvation. I receive it in a new and fresh way from you and I declare that nothing can separate me now from the love of Christ and the place I shall ever have in your kingdom. *(Helmet of salvation section)*

Holy Spirit, show me specifically today the truths of the Word of God that I will need to counter the assaults and the snares of the Enemy. Bring them to mind throughout the day. *(The sword of the Spirit – which is the word of God section)*

Finally, Holy Spirit, I agree to walk in step with you in everything — in all prayer as my spirit communes with you throughout the day. *(Alertness section – always keep praying for all the saints)*[6]

---

6. Taken from *Wild at Heart* by John Eldredge Copyright © 2001 John Eldredge. Used by permission of Thomas Nelson. www.thomasnelson.com. *Compiled by Daniel Flagg 7/22/2007*

90. Fear Not

The author of First John 4:18 says, "There is no fear in love. But perfect love drives out fear, because fear has to do with punishment. The one who fears is not made perfect in love."

My *Life Application Bible* has this note related to this verse in 1st John: "If we ever are afraid of the future, eternity or God's judgment, we can remind ourselves of God's love. We know that he loves us perfectly. That is what Romans 8:38 & 39 declare, "For I am convinced that neither death nor life, neither angels nor demons, neither the present nor the future, nor any powers, neither height nor depth, nor anything else in all creation, will be able to separate us from the love of God that is in Christ Jesus our Lord."

Recently, I was on a phone conversation with a person that I have mentored over the years. This individual was distraught over several things going on in her life, and I sensed that she was giving power to the enemy in this situation because I heard a phrase that I had heard from her in fear before. This phrase was "I can't."

Fortunately, I recognized this as a problem from previous discussions and addressed this fear with her. I encouraged her and informed her that the enemy wanted her to believe that she couldn't and that the enemy had power over her as long as she believed that.

However, that is not the truth found in the Bible. In Philippians 4:13 it says, "I can do everything through him who gives me strength." So I told her that she can, that this thing that she thought had a hold on her was not of God and that she just needs to claim the promises of God and renounce this thing.

She recognized that this was a trap that she had fallen into before. I immediately heard the uncertainty in her voice disappear in exchange for a newfound peace and calm. Sometimes that is all we need. We need to remember that God does not want us to be paralyzed by our fears, but to claim the promises of God and renounce whatever it is that is bringing us the fear.

91. Hearing God

Whose voice is it you hear in the solitude of your home or during the chaos of a hectic day? Although these moments are opportunities for us to hear from God, unfortunately, during some of these times we seem to hear the voice of the enemy. Satan strives to speak to us and tell us things which are contrary to the Word of God.

Because Satan is the master of all lies, He competes for the space in our heads with the truth which comes from Jesus. One of the keys to overcoming the enemy is to utilize a battlefield mindset. 2 Corinthians 10:5 states that as Christians, "We demolish arguments and every pretension that sets itself up against the knowledge of God, and we take captive every thought to make it obedient to Christ." The instruction to "take every thought captive" employs the battlefield mindset in order to combat Satan's deceit so that we may hear the truth of God.

While listening to a Christian radio station, I began ruminating on this thought. I quickly realized the power of our thoughts and the ability to quickly turn them around in the name of God. Whenever we catch ourselves believing the lies of the enemy we need to stop and twist the words around to glorify God. With this thought, I wrote this poem entitled "Hearing God."

Hearing God

I cannot go on, this is way too much
I've lost control, I'm out of touch
I cannot do it, I am nothing
I am powerless, I'll never be something
I have no power, all I see is defeat
No strength in me, no strength in these feet
I am going backwards, I can't turn it around
My friends despise me and my foes abound
All is lost, there is nothing to hang on for

Should I take my life or just lay on the floor
I am useless, I have nothing to live for
I can't, I won't, there is nothing more
But wait I hear something - is that you God
Yes you say, my thoughts are all flawed
I can do all things through Christ who strengthens me
Well Glory to God, by all means let it be
Satan I will not take your apple
No I am going straight to the chapel
For you hold no power over me
Jesus is in me and now I can see
With Jesus in me you are a defeated foe
So get out of here and on with the show
Jesus is King let the parade begin
He rules in me you can never come in
I am a new creation, no longer bound to sin
The Holy Spirit now resides within
He paid it all with His blood on the cross
Now I will make Him my all-time greatest boss.

92. Hope

"For everything that was written in the past was written to teach us, so that through endurance and the encouragement of the Scriptures we might have hope."
Romans 15:4

For Christians, hope comes from the Scriptures, from reading the Word. Notice the inclusion of the words "endurance" and "encouragement." I find it significant that prior this in Romans 5:3-4, it reads: "Not only so, but we also rejoice in our sufferings, because we know that suffering produces perseverance; perseverance, character; and character, hope.

Could this be where the reference to endurance comes from — that we must endure suffering? So steadfast hope is not achieved overnight. Often it is achieved by experiencing suffering, which leads to perseverance. Through persevering over time we develop character, and over time, as our character is built up, so is our hope.

Our encouragement of the Scriptures to help us endure the sufferings is Jesus Christ. For it is written in John 1:1: "In the beginning was the Word, and the Word was with God, and the Word was God." This means Jesus was present at the beginning of time with God, and He is referred to as the living Word. Jesus, as a part of the Holy Trinity, is God. So through reading the Scriptures, both the Old Testament and the New Testament, we have fellowship with Christ; we are communing with our Almighty Savior. What a great gift we have in the Word!

Romans 15:4 says: "For everything that was written in the past was written to teach us." Yes, Jesus is the Great Teacher, and we can grow wiser by reading His Word. And, simultaneously, whether we are feeling lonely or fantastic, reading the Word, especially in times of despair, can turn our despair into hope. When we take time for devotion, to spend time in the Word, we learn – for God is teaching us His ways. I believe the best time to do this is first thing in the morning.

As we learn, we develop in our hope, so that our hope cannot be changed. Our hope becomes like God, who does not change but is the same every day. Oh, that we would develop that type of spirituality through reading the Word, that we might stand firm, rather than being tossed and blown by the wind, as many do who cleave to the world's ways rather than His ways. Lord, help us to cleave to You and Your Word.

93. A Bright Light for a Dark World

Are you a bright light in a dark, fallen world? God calls us to be salt and light to this dark world. We should be a beacon of light, like a lighthouse that serves as a guiding light and reference point to ships passing by in the ocean. God wants us to be a guiding light for those who have lost or are unsure of their way. The truth of God found in the Word should be our reference to guide us in helping those around us.

When we study the Word of God, we are studying truth — the powerful truth of God revealed through His Word. The Word leads us into truth and changes us, and we will never be the same when the truth of God is held up against the lies of this dark world. God will use us to bring about change in the world when we are knowledgeable about the Bible and what God stands for.

Once I was able to help someone out who was contemplating divorce by using the truth of the word of God. I had grown to know this person and was informed that they were contemplating leaving their spouse. Because of my past problems in my marriage, I wanted to share with this person my journey and how love won out in our marriage. I reached out and spoke with this person and shared Lisa's and my story with him.

Then, after talking further, I asked him if I could read Deuteronomy 28 to him. In this chapter, detailed descriptions of the blessings that God anoints us with for obedience are described, along with graphic descriptions of the curses that will come upon us for disobedience.

I also had recently heard a sermon message relating to this struggle over divorce, and arranged to get this sermon in CD form so this person could listen to it. Because the marriage was saved, I feel like God used me to reach out and help this person, and God used that to save their marriage.

This is what being a Christian is all about being a bright light of hope in a dark world, to reach out and help others in their time of need. We see Christian groups do this after times of natural disasters in various countries throughout the world, and we see Christians doing this locally in their own community.

When we seek God and are open to doing His will, and ask Him to guide us we can do great things with Him. Pray that God will show you those circumstances where you can be salt and light to those who may be in a difficult situations, where God can get the glory.

94. Do Not Criticize

Do you realize that when we criticize we are going against God's Word? In Ephesians 4:29 we are told, "Do not let any unwholesome talk come out of your mouths, but only what is helpful for building others up according to their needs, that it may benefit those who listen."

In James 4:11 the same idea is conveyed but in one short concise statement: "Brothers, do not slander one another." From Colossians it is conveyed in a more positive loving spirit. In Colossians 4:6, the apostle Paul writes, "Let your conversation be always full of grace, seasoned with salt, so that you may know how to answer everyone."

Let's explore why it is so important not to criticize. Let's try and grasp the importance of guarding our tongues and only speaking uplifting words to one another, as we are encouraged to do throughout the Bible.

I heard one pastor say that criticism breaks our fellowship with the Holy Spirit. It is so important not to criticize because we cannot be blessed by the Holy Spirit when we go against God's Word.

To give a more dramatic example, if a family is in the middle of their devotion time (where the Holy Spirit is present), and one of the family members gets up and hits another, this action will abruptly change the atmosphere within the room—and the fellowship with the Holy Spirit will be broken.

While we may not realize it, if the same family were in their devotional time together and out of the blue a stinging criticism was spoken by one family member against another, again, it will also break their fellowship with the Holy Spirit.

Both the physical fight and the verbal abuse brings conflict into the meeting, instead of the unity which God desires. Every form of criticism breaks the fellowship with the Holy Spirit. When we criticize someone, we are acting apart from the character of God and the Holy Spirit. We cannot be simultaneously filled with the Holy Spirit and be critical. If the

Holy Spirit were present in us prior to the criticism, the Holy Spirit will leave when we criticize.

Have you ever been at a dinner table where everyone is genteel and the discussions are warm and then someone speaks an insult or criticism towards someone else at the table? We have probably all experienced this and understand how awkward it becomes. No one knows what to say because this criticism had changed the entire atmosphere around the dinner table. Usually someone will change the conversation to the weather or something else. But if the person being criticized returns the criticism to the perpetrator, then the argument escalates and becomes even more heated.

Fortunately, not only does the Word of God reveal to us that we are not to criticize, but it also tells us what we should do—build others up with supportive language or compliments. Encouragement brings glory to God and the Holy Spirit can fan the flames of the Spirit present in us.

So let us practice uplifting words of affirmation to one another and in doing so God will change our hearts. As is stated above, we will know how we should respond in every situation and how we ought to answer everyone. Then God will be glorified through the building up of another rather than tearing down another.

95. Don't Sweat the Small Stuff

In this life there are many events that happen on a daily basis that can exasperate us. And yet God wants us to be unshaken by the things of this world. Sure, God wants us to employ intercessory prayer for the troubling issues in today's world—the poor, war, greed, abortion and sexual immorality. But we know that in this world we will have trouble, and our place as Christians is to remain steadfast in our faith and focused on our Savior, Jesus.

With the goal of remaining steadfast in our faith, it is important that we remain grounded—unmoved by the things of this world—particularly regarding the "small stuff."

If we let our mind drift or be pulled out of focus where we become unbalanced on even the smaller things, then it will be that much harder to remain "on track" and do the things that God calls us to do when larger obstacles confront us. I see it as a mental mindset that God uses.

As the fruit of the Spirit overflows from our lives and spills into the lives of others, our optimism, our joy, our love, our peace, our patience, our kindness, our gentleness and our enthusiasm for life overflows and spills into the lives of others to accomplish God's perfect will.

We must fight to maintain this mindset, no matter what the enemy throws at us, and we need to remain vigilant to preserve this favorable disposition and outlook in our mind. When we do not do this—when we let each little thing pile up and become like an insurmountable obstacle— we begin losing the battle in our minds and create openings for depression to set in.

How do we avoid letting the small stuff get us down? As I think of how to overcome this ongoing battle, I think of those in my life who are always optimistic. They seem to be the ones with a happy go lucky mindset; they never let the little things get in the way. I think of the people who are "can do" people, those who take action.

They appear as strong stalwarts that are ready to tackle any obstacle, and they believe nothing is impossible. They also realize they have prevailed in the past, and they are not daunted by ordinary obstacles that we all face in everyday life. Beyond the spiritual factors of reading the Bible and praying regularly, these individuals seem to have grit—a desire to conquer and succeed—and they don't seem to get down. It appears to be an acquired mindset.

Once they get to that place in their mind where they are ready to tackle the issues of everyday life, they hold onto that mindset. We all know people like this and if we are trying to attain the peace and confidence they exhibit, perhaps the best approach is to study their actions. We can pray that God will guide us in mimicking the positive actions we see in these individuals, realizing the battle ground is in our heads. May you endeavor to find that place where you feel confident and peaceful in handling the small issues on a daily basis. And then you can enjoy life more and be more useful to God as you avoid despair and "don't sweat the small stuff."

96. Praise Him, Praise Him, Praise Him

It might seem strange to include this gold nugget on praising God within this section on overcoming Satan's attacks. Typically we think of overcoming the power of Satan through putting on the full armor of God as listed in the sixth chapter of Ephesians or perhaps gathering with others in prayer to come against the Enemy's attacks. But there is tremendous power in praising God; it can be a game changer, especially when we are under attack.

I believe one of the reasons there is so much power in praising God during periods of demonic attack is because Satan expects that we will falter or be shaken. However we can turn this around on the Enemy by being unshaken and instead praising God during times of adversity. We become overcomers, when we learn to overcome what we previously succumbed to and were shaken by. As we grow in our faith we can recognize the tactics of the enemy and have a set game plan to overcome these schemes.

One of the best game plans, when you recognize an attack, is to begin praising God. Satan wants to separate us from the love of God, but we know through Paul's writing in Romans that we are more than conquerors. We can turn the tables on Satan and overcome His attacks. This is written in Romans 8:35, 37: "Who shall separate us from love of Christ? Shall trouble or hardship or persecution or famine or nakedness or danger or sword? No, in all these things we are more than conquerors through Him who loved us." And we can conquer by praising God.

I experienced just such a turn-around, I became an overcomer one day in November of 2016. It was a Saturday and I had felt spiritual attacks all day long. Nothing seemed to go right and my wife and I had been argumentative all day. I wrote in my journal at midnight that night that the spiritual attacks I felt that day were the strongest I had felt in months, but I resolved to end the day on a high note, to praise God. I decided to document my praises in my journal, that although the day was a difficult day, I would record in my journal all the praises and thanks I could think of. Because that day had gone badly I began by praising Him for the day before (Friday) and I recalled many blessings from that day and praised and thanked God for each one in writing in my journal.

Through this it changed my heart and mind and I began to think of things I could praise God for that day. Many of these hadn't gone well but I wrote that I was thankful I was nonetheless able to get a lot accomplished. Then I went back over the last month or so and praised God for his faithfulness, for all the blessings and answered prayers He had provided. Finally, I praised God for the events upcoming in the future and stated that I trusted that they would go well (including my daughter's wedding the next month).

God confirmed that He was pleased with my praise of Him that night and early the next morning. He did this by awakening me with a prophetic dream about this book. I got up immediately and wrote it down and tried to go back to sleep. I could not fall back to sleep but over the next hour, before I would normally get up to get ready for prayer time before church, I experienced two prophetic visions concerning this book. Then in our small prayer room where the prayer team prays before church the Holy Spirit was vividly present. I prayed with emotion and cried at two points while praying as I was overcome with the Holy Spirit. I was full of power and enthusiasm on only four and one half hours of sleep, undoubtedly the work of the Holy Spirit in this body, which is used to six to seven hours of sleep.

I believe God wants us always to be overcomers, to resolve to stay the course over setbacks both large and small. I experienced this on a smaller issue when I had a flat tire one day. I had a great day and was looking forward to going to our small group meeting that night. I pulled into my garage after work, about 20 minutes before small group was due to start.

I unpacked and changed and went back to my car to depart for small group and saw that I had a flat tire. But rather than say "Oh I don't have time to change the tire and get to small group," I resolved to not only change the tire, but to praise Him as I changed the tire. I was able to get it changed quickly and arrived at small group in a positive state of mind only a few minutes late. I encourage you to resolve to overcome all of the issues that the Enemy throws at you, both large and small. Continuing to praise God through the battles is just one way to be an overcomer, but this combined with the full armor of God and prayer is strong and powerful in the arms of believers.

Concluding
Gold Nuggets

97. The Decision of a Lifetime

Have you ever heard the saying, "One 'Oh Crap' wipes out 100 'Atta-boys'"? This is a common premise in this world. Even if you do one hundred good things the world or your boss is waiting for you to make that one mistake, and it wipes out all the good things done previously.

I find that to be particularly true in this ultracompetitive world in which we live today. In the high profile cases like football coaches or corporate bosses, one bad season or one bad financial year can be your undoing. So that is how this works in the material world. But the reverse is true with God.

God offers us eternal life at any point in our life, regardless of what we have done previously and regardless of the number of times we have sinned. Like a good father, God forgives us for everything out of His love and mercy. He accepts us without reservation.

This one decision to accept Christ's free gift of salvation wipes out one hundred or more mistakes. Because Jesus paid for our sin, God accepts us as we are when we surrender our lives to Him. There is nothing too big, nothing too bad to keep us from the love of God.

The decision to accept Jesus as our personal Lord and Savior, and surrender all for Him is definitely the decision of a lifetime. So we don't have to worry about this world and our past. All we have to do is sincerely submit to Him and desire to walk with Him all the days of our life. What a merciful and loving father God is. Thanks be to God!

98. Christian Dance

My eldest daughter, Kaitlyn, danced in a Christian dance company from the age of 9 until she graduated high school. So I thought I would treat you to a dance performance of Christian singer Nicol Sponberg's song, Resurrection, performed by En Pointe Dance Academy in 2009. Kaitlyn is the lead dancer dressed in black in this performance, captured by Green Peas Productions. I hope that it will be as much of a blessing to you to watch this video as it has been to me. This performance was posted to YouTube and you can view it by typing this web address into your computer or phone.

https://www.youtube.com/
watch?v=naNCgpCVODk&feature=share_email

Also this particular dance academy was a blessing to our entire family, especially Kaitlyn, as she would have devotion time every Thursday night during the dance practices. I don't know if all Christian dance companies are run like this one, but if you have a daughter who is a dancer, you may want to try to find a Christian dance company where she experiences Bible time incorporated with her dance time.

99. Heaven or Hell?

As I am writing this gold nugget, I need to take you back and reflect on the purpose of this book. The intent is to provide you, the reader, with thoughts and experiences from my life, which might serve as motivation to make changes in your life.

The expectation is that these changes would be positive changes, resulting in a closer walk with God that would bless you in the process. The revelation to write this book came straight from God during my devotion time one morning, and I am following what I heard from God that morning.

The scriptural basis behind this book and my encounter with God that morning is John 10:10—"I have come that they may have life, and have it to the full." As the title of this book implies, I presume the vast majority of the readers are Christians and that they desire their relationship with God to be elevated, which God desires for each of us.

My purpose in writing it is to encourage you to develop a closer walk with God. And if you are not a believer, may you be encouraged to accept Jesus Christ as your Savior—the only way to obtain eternal life in heaven.

I would be remiss as a Christian and a writer, if I did not draw attention to the fact that contrary to public sentiment not everyone that believes there is a heaven will necessarily end up in heaven. There are many casual Christians and believers of other faiths that believe in heaven. But Jesus was clear during His time on earth that many will be locked out of heaven

If they are locked out of heaven that means they will be condemned to hell. They will not experience eternal life in heaven in fellowship with God the Father and Jesus Christ, as well as the hosts in heaven. This grieves my heart. It grieves my heart that many will trade a life apart from God on earth for less than one hundred years, and miss out on the blessings of heaven for eternity.

Life in heaven will be infinitely better than life on earth and yet many, if not most of creation, will not experience the beauty, majesty, peace and glory of heaven. How peaceful it will be to experience life in heaven where there is no more pain, no more crying, no more death or mourning, but rather abundant joy and praising of our Father and Creator of heaven and earth.

But again, many—if not most, who have lived a relatively short time on earth compared to an eternity in heaven—will not experience heaven.

The words of Jesus tell us so in Luke 13, 23-27.

> Someone asked him, "Lord, are only a few people going to be saved?"
>
> "He said to them, 'Make every effort to enter through the narrow door, because many, I tell you, will try to enter and will not be able to. Once the owner of the house gets up and closes the door, you will stand outside knocking and pleading, "Sir, open the door for us. But he will answer, 'I don't know you or where you come from." Then you will say, 'We ate and drank with you, and you taught in our streets.' But he will reply, 'I don't know you or where you come from. Away from me, all you evildoers!'

In this passage the owner of the house refers to God the Father of heaven and earth, and in this lesson Jesus is telling us that the Father of heaven will have many come to the door of heaven but they won't be able to enter because they are evildoers.

If evildoers will not enter heaven it is paramount that we obtain a good understanding of who they are. Evildoers are the ones whom succumb to the schemes and tactics of the evil one, Satan.

This seems reasonable but is it possible that some churchgoers, some who believe in heaven might be considered evildoers, and also be locked out of heaven. The answer is found in Matthew 5:20, "For I tell you that unless your righteousness surpasses that of the Pharisees and the teachers of the law, you will certainly not enter the kingdom of heaven."

Again, Jesus is speaking here and informs us that many who think they are religious, even those who read the Bible, will not enter the kingdom of heaven unless they are righteous. Many think they are righteous, and they may be in their eyes, but we need to grasp that we must be viewed as righteous by the perfect God of the Universe. Are we really righteous in His eyes?

Another Scripture regarding this is 1 Corinthians 6:9. This passage reads, "Do you not know that the wicked will not inherit the kingdom of God? Do not be deceived: Neither the sexually immoral nor idolaters nor adulterers nor male prostitutes nor homosexual offenders [10] nor thieves nor the greedy nor drunkards nor slanderers nor swindlers will inherit the kingdom of God."

Many think they are good Christians but they may be getting drunk regularly, or may be greedy or idolaters, or slanderers and gossipers. Jesus tells us in these verses that they will not enter the kingdom of heaven. Notice the descriptive words used in this verse. It does not say someone who has been drunk, it does not say someone who once swindled another.

The terms used such as idolaters, drunkards, slanderers all indicate a present state where the person is continuing to practice this sin repeatedly, up until their time of death. So, everyone who once committed these sins, and through God's grace has accepted Christ as their Lord and Savior and are being transformed through Jesus Christ *will* inherit the kingdom of God.

For those that are reading these words for the first time, and God touches their heart and lays open for them to see the sin of their ways, you can turn to God now and be saved. You can have eternal life with the Father in heaven if you renounce your sinful ways.

You must acknowledge your sin, ask to be forgiven of your sin, and tell God that you believe that Jesus Christ died for your sins and that you are ready to accept that fact and follow Jesus (…all the way to heaven). God desires that none should perish.

He desires that all would turn to Jesus when they are exposed to the truth that apart from Jesus they will not be able to experience life in heaven. And so, everyone is free to turn to Jesus for everlasting life. But as we read in the Bible, many will never do it. God tells us in John 14:6, "I am the way and the truth and the life. No one comes to the Father (heaven) except through me."

My hope is that everyone reading this book will join me and other believers in Jesus Christ in heaven. My prayer for each reader is that the Holy Spirit will penetrate your soul through the reading of this book and that if you are not a Christian that you will surrender your life to Jesus and join Him in heaven with our God and Father. And lest you still need a prompting—a word to spur you to take action—consider finally the words of Jesus Christ as written in Matthew 7:13-14. These words were spoken by Jesus, "Enter through the narrow gate. For wide is the gate and broad is the road that leads to destruction, and many enter through it. But small is the gate and narrow the road that leads to life, and only a few find it." I pray that you will be one of the few!

100. Get Closer to Heaven

We are here at the end—gold nugget 100. In gold nugget 99 I put forth God's position that although He created each of us, only a minority will enter heaven. And in Luke 13:24, Jesus told us to, "<u>Make every effort</u> to enter the narrow door."

That is the entire focus of this book, to inspire and encourage you to develop a closer walk with God. Whether you are an "on fire" Christian, a "casual" Christian, or a non-Christian who was somehow led to this book, my hope is that this book spurred you on to practice many of the ideas and strategies contained in the 100 gold nuggets.

The key to any learning is not to stop at reading it, but to put it into practice. Jesus told those around Him they would be His disciples—not if they simply *listened* to His commands, but if they *followed* His commandments.

In this final gold nugget, I want to suggest activities to move beyond where you are now in your relationship with God. I want to suggest ways to rise up towards Heaven and embrace God's plan for you. God has inspired me to include 12 mini nuggets—12 suggestions which will be a step in the right direction, if you will practice them individually.

If several of these mini nuggets are employed, or all of them are begun, it should catapult your walk with God and dramatically change your life. Undoubtedly many of you are already practicing several of these mini nuggets, but perhaps one or more of the remaining nuggets will grab your attention and complement your current repertoire. If you are not practicing any of these activities, I suggest you start with one or two and see how God leads you from there.

Mini-Nugget #1 – Before getting out of bed, pray for one thing you want God to do. Beginning with Day 2, believe He answered your prayer on Day 1. Thank God in various ways for 28 days.

Mini-Nugget #2 – Print out and read over your top ten prayers each day for a month. Scratch out or write "answered" across your answered prayers during the month.

Mini-Nugget #3 – Speak an encouraging word to one person each and every day.

Mini-Nugget #4 – Give a small amount of cash once per week to one homeless person, street person, or person in need.

Mini-Nugget #5 – Pray a short prayer (in silence) for one stranger each day that you walk by or see, but do not speak to.

Mini-Nugget #6 – Volunteer once a month at a charity or non-profit organization.

Mini-Nugget #7 – Pray for your immediate family's unity, love and joy each day.

Mini-Nugget #8 – Go into the woods (or park if you live in a city) once per month and seek God for a couple of hours.

Mini-Nugget #9 – Fast for one meal once per week and fast with an intention of offering it up for a specific purpose each week.

Mini-Nugget #10 – Tell one person each week that you have committed to pray for them once a day during that week. Then ask them what they would like you to pray for.

Mini-Nugget #11 – Talk about God with one stranger once per week. This may seem hard, but try something easy like saying, "Isn't God good?" If they agree you can expound. If they answer, "No," that is a door opening for you to display compassion. Perhaps, by asking them why they feel that way they will open up about a need in their life, which you can try to assist them with.

Mini-Nugget #12 – Near the end of every week, (i.e. on Saturday), make a list of 10 things to praise God for that happened that week and write them down in a journal.

About the Author

Daniel Flagg was born in Atlanta, Georgia, and has lived in the Atlanta area for all but five years of his life. He always had a strong faith, but it became alive with a personal connection to Jesus when he surrendered his life to Christ in 2003.

In 2017, Daniel felt a great burden to begin praying for the lost in Atlanta, and founded Atlanta Prayer Partners. He was serving on the prayer team at church, but felt a passion to step outside the walls of the church to intercede with others for Atlanta and the nation. In August of 2017, Atlanta Prayer Partners began gathering monthly at gateways and historic locations around Atlanta.

This burden of prayer took on a larger scope in 2018 after he met David Burgher of Bridge the Gap Ministries at the National Day of Prayer. Mr. Burgher invited Daniel to join the board of Directors of his ministry and to expand the prayer gatherings to courthouses around Atlanta.

As this vision has unfolded, they have seen God's favor on their gatherings in Atlanta. Individuals with cancer and other physical ailments who were walking by have joined them in the prayers. Daniel believes they will see many come to faith in Christ as well as miraculous healings at these prayer gatherings as those walking by join them in fellowship and prayer.

Daniel is self-employed as a home inspector and lives with his wife, Lisa, who is a teacher in the suburbs of Atlanta. He and Lisa have three grown children and two grandchildren, and cherish family time with all of them.

CPSIA information can be obtained
at www.ICGtesting.com
Printed in the USA
FFHW011615101218
49809084-54363FF